SOME GODDESSES
GODDESSES
Of the Pen

SOME GODDESSES
Of the Pen

BY

PATRICK BRAYBROOKE
Fellow of the Royal Society of Literature

Essay Index Reprint Series

BOOKS FOR LIBRARIES PRESS, INC.
FREEPORT, NEW YORK

FIRST PUBLISHED 1928
REPRINTED 1966

Printed In The United States of America

DEDICATION

TO BERYL AND NIGEL

(Without their Permission)

PREFACE

Writing of my companion volume, " Novelists, We Are Seven " the Literary Critic of *The New York World* used the following expressions of opinion.

" Mr. Braybrooke adopts the best and simplest method of criticism that of picking out some definite salient feature which in each portrays the writer through his own eyes as a mirror to the public. There is no criticism easier and pleasanter for the public to accept."

In this present book, which concerns some well-konwn writers, I have attempted the same method as that commented on above.

In my choice of these women writers I have been guided by one principle. I have endeavoured to select those who are most diverse one from the other.

If any one is foolish enough to attempt to compare the eight women writers with an idea of determining which of them is most " without spot or blemish," he will find that comparisons are not only odious, but have a nasty habit of violating the sanest principle of Literary Criticism—that a thing should be judged in so far as it achieves that which it has attempted to achieve.

PATRICK BRAYBROOKE.

1 *Leinster Square, Hyde Park.*
    Easter, 1927.

CONTENTS

PART ONE
MISS SHEILA KAYE-SMITH

MISS SHEILA KAYE-SMITH
Press Portrait Bureau.

PART ONE

MISS SHEILA KAYE-SMITH

It is perhaps a little melancholy to have to record the fact that a good deal of Miss Kaye-Smith's work is grim. There is certain enjoyment discernible in this grimness, as though the author took pleasure in revealing that side of life which is hard and utterly uncompromising. I find this hard strain very evident in one of Miss Kaye-Smith's most noteworthy books, " The End of the House of Alard." But let it be said at once, and said quite emphatically, that the grimness of the story is a very good reason for the high artistic level of this particular work. It may be that it is in large part the background of " The End of the House of Alard " that postulates the austerity of the story. The open country, by its very contempt of man, is naturally reserved and austere, unconcerned, callous, and this atmosphere logically conveys itself to Miss Kaye-Smith.

On her title page Miss Kaye-Smith lets us know that we are likely to experience something sad and sombre in this book, for she very aptly quotes thus from Mr. Chesterton :

" We only know that the last sad squires ride slowly
towards the sea,
And a new people takes the land."

By means of a discussion concerning certain elements in " The End of The House of Alard " I hope to be able to write, though in very slight detail, something of the capable art of Miss Kaye-Smith

. . . .

Quite early on in her story, Miss Kaye-Smith writes a characteristic description of what marriage means to a woman. Her creation of Stella Mount may be perhaps among the most skilfully drawn of her women characters, or, shall I say, of the creation of women of the " lady " type. I do not imagine that many women would disagree with what Miss Kaye-Smith makes Stella think to herself about the first rapture of complete possession that is the logical consequence of marriage. Stella is thinking about the ecstasy of being in " bondage " to Peter Alard. She thinks in this admirable manner.

" On her face, on her neck, she could still feel cold places where Peter had kissed her. It was wonderful, she thought, that she should carry the ghosts of his kisses through Sussex and Kent. She would see Peter again soon, and the time would come—must come— when they would be together always."

It carries Stella, a most charming person, into a delicious day dream. Delicious as are all day dreams.

" They were married and together always," sounded better in her ears than " they married and lived happy ever after."

So Stella progresses in her day dream, and we are glad that this girl has it, for it will not be so long before Miss Kaye-Smith shows the awakening from the dream, an awakening that would have made Stella wish she could dream for ever and ever.

" No more partings, no more ghosts of kisses, much as she loved those ghosts, but always the dear warm bodily presence—Peter working, Peter resting, Peter sleepy, Peter hungry, Peter talking, Peter silent—Peter always."

In dealing with the characters in " The End of The House of Alard," Miss Kaye-Smith adopts, for the most part, a rather detached attitude to them. Perhaps this is a very marked characteristic of her art. Yet, and this is the clever dualism of the author, though she is detached from her characters, Miss Kaye-Smith invests them with the warm attributes of flesh and blood. Her characters possess more than anything else, an excellent degree of naturalness. Possibly in this way Miss Kaye-Smith gives us the key to her well-deserved popularity and her high position in the world of fiction writers. There seems to be very little conscious effort about her; we feel that once the tale is started, the author has merely followed an easy passage until the last word is written. Particularly is this so in the book I am writing of. " The End of The House of Alard " moves with a delightful ease ; it has an easy air of conscripting the reader's attention without making him a little angry ; that conscription has been applied to his attention.

Through the whole of the book we are made to feel sorry for the Alards ; they are the participators in such an unequal fight. They fight an internal relentless foe, they seem to demonstrate the absolute truism, that we can usually fight anything and anybody with some chance of success, except *ourselves*. The end of the noble house of Alard is brought about by the Alards. It is in this that Miss Kaye-Smith harps on the tragic, for of all the tragedies that pursue a family, the most tragic is that tragedy which makes a family, as it were, end itself. There is a bitter picture of Gervase Alard looking back to the religious faith of his childhood. The bitterness that it is all gone, the horrid feeling, that would seem to have been shared by Hood in one of his most exquisite poems. That sensation of getting farther and farther away which Hood puts so pathetically when he writes :

> I remember, I remember,
> The fir trees dark and high
> I used to think their tender tops
> Were close against the sky :
> It was a childish ignorance,
> But now 'tis little joy
> To know I'm farther off from heaven
> Than when I was a boy.

There is a distinct parallel to this when Miss Kaye-Smith allows Gervase Alard to ruminate on his boyhood's religion.

" He must have been a queer sort of kid. Now all that was gone : religion—the school chapel, confirmation classes, manly Christians, the Bishop's sleeves."

Then there is the melancholy aftermath. Miss Kaye-Smith puts it very concisely and accurately.

" Religion was so different after you were grown up. It became an affair of earth and halfpence, like everything else."

With a good deal of insight the religion of Stella Mount is contrasted with the non-religion of Gervase Alard. The woman is able to retain something of the beliefs she held when she was a child. Does Miss Kaye-Smith imply by this that she considers women retain their " young " religious outlook more often than men ? If she does, I think her contention open to objection. But in this Essay I am merely concerned at the moment, in the contrast in outlook between Stella Mount and Gervase Alard. This is how the girl's religion strikes Gervase.

" Stella's religion still seemed to have some colour left in it, some life, some youth. It was more like his childhood's faith than anything he had met so far. She had told him that she never thought of Christ as being born in Bethlehem, but in the barn at the back of the Plough Inn at Udimore."

In " The End of The House of Alard " the author deals with that essential kind of culture which the unthinking are very prone to call pure and simple snobbery. The head of that most worthy house is delightfully drawn. Miss Kaye-Smith almost uncannily gets at the disgust of Sir John that his sons should so degrade themselves as to earn any money ! Miss Kaye-Smith brings out this rather typical characteristic when she describes the reception that Gervase gets at the hands of his father, when he brings in the first earned money to wit, no less than five whole and intact shillings.

" The sarcasm that greeted his first return on Saturday afternoon with his five shillings in his pocket was equalled only by his own pride."

Sir John is naturally irritated, for the earning of such money is something that is the beginning of the end, or at

least the beginning of a new point of view, and old aris-
tocrats do not readily accept new points of view. They
are scornful of conservatism, the backbone and mainstay
of aristocracy.

> " We can launch out a bit now," said Sir John at
> luncheon. " Gervase has come to our rescue, and is
> supporting us in our hour of need."

Again this culture or snobbery of the Alard's is brought
out pungently enough when Stella remarks that the
Alard's are not poor, as they keep so many motor cars and
servants. But that is exactly why they are poor. They
cannot adapt themselves. Perhaps Miss Kaye-Smith is
a little hard on the old people, for it is morally impossible
for certain people to realise that new conditions have
arrived, that old boats must be burned, that life must
continue, but continue along a different path ; a path,
it may be, choked with thorns, where it had been decked
with sweet-smelling roses. Peter voices all youth's contempt for those parents who will not change, but he for-
gets that they *cannot* change, without a violent process of
looking at life from a completely new aspect.

> " Oh, that's my hopeless parents, who won't give up
> anything they've been accustomed to, and who say that
> it's not worth while making ourselves uncomfortable
> in small things when only something colossal can save
> us. If we moved into the Lodge to-morrow and lived
> on five hundred a year it would still take us more than
> a lifetime to scrape up enough to free the land."

And it would be just as useful to ask Sir John to live
on a hundred a year as to expect him to suddenly descend

to the plebeian level of five hundred a year. Miss Kaye-Smith is of course laughing at the inexorable obstinacy of the Alard House, which is bringing about its own inevitable ruin. But it is far easier to tell people that they should live on a reduced income than to be the people to whom the unpleasant information is imparted. Old people are seldom adaptable, and Miss Kaye-Smith emphasises this truth very much by the example of the House of Alard.

.   .   .   .

Miss Kaye-Smith has a clever way of creating dialogue that deals with difficult questions, and she is particularly good at showing the difference in the masculine and feminine point of view with regard to a problem that is both sordid and delicate. The example of this art, that I quote, is where Sir John and Lady Alard argue about the disquieting but popular practice of adultery. Always an unpleasant subject, because adultery, sometimes harmless enough in itself, brings out all the self-complacency in those admirable people who are perfectly moral for fear of the consequences.

Adultery comes to the Alard family with something of the shock that such an event has on all family's which consider themselves free from the ordinary weaknesses of mankind. Miss Kaye-Smith seems to be a little shocked and annoyed by the self-satisfaction of the Alard family.

" Peter was genuinely shocked—the Alards did not appear in the divorce court."

Sir John, while admitting that adultery is a " nasty mess," has no dislike of talking about it quite openly in front of his wife and daughters The dialogue is again natural and reasonable.

" ' That would be a nasty mess, wouldn't it, sir ?' said Peter.

" ' Not such a nasty mess as my daughter being held up in all the newspapers as an adulteress ! '

" ' Oh, John !' cried Lady Alard, ' what a dreadful thing to say before the girls.' "

There is a good deal of perception in these remarks. There is a certain weakness about Lady Alard, a vague temerity which makes her quail before her bullying and authoritative husband. Sir John Alard cares for nothing really except his good name ; Lady Alard is more concerned for the morals of her daughters. Miss Kaye-Smith brings out the fundamental difference in viewpoint with discrimination and skill. She shows again and again in her works this understanding of the eternal difference that persists and always will persist between the two sexes. It is this understanding that makes her fiction so valuable and created with such a lively realisation of human nature. Sir John is perturbed about the adultery of one of his daughters from purely selfish motives, the dragging down of his good name; Lady Alard is chiefly upset that such a thing should happen to one of her own children. It is the everlasting and essential unselfishness of motherhood.

I shall proceed some distance to another incident in the history of this unfortunate Alard family. It concerns the death of George Alard, the son of the family who is a clergyman, not perhaps a brilliant priest, but a typical clergyman trying to live up to his high calling and trying to do something for that much-abused body The Church of England, that Church which, always said to be dying, pertinaciously is quite optimistic of Eternal Life.

I think on careful consideration that the description of the death of George Alard has a right to be selected as a fine piece of writing and a picture of the art of Miss Kaye Smith at her best.

There is nothing so easy for a novelist as to exaggerate when writing of any real and essentially deep moment in life. The description of many death scenes written by novelists give the impression of a very conscious effort to produce something highly melodramatic. They appear to be written with more regard for drama than for truth, perhaps very largely because some novelists do not seem to realise that death is drama and need never be *made* into drama. A death scene should work out its own salvation, it should take the situation in its own hands and lead the novelist along, very gently it may be, or with a violence that may leave him terrified and exhausted.

I think that the reason Miss Kaye-Smith has written such a fine and moving picture of the death of George Alard, is that she has allowed the scene to work its own way through. The author gets all the confusion of sudden death, the frantic ringings of bells, the hurried calling of a sleeping house into activity, the desperate attempt to stave off death by the calling in of a doctor, the terrible coming of the priest and the last preparations to send forth the soul equipped with some kind of spiritual and metaphysical armour.

I hope that a fairly lengthy quotation will make it clear that Miss Kaye-Smith does not exaggerate, nor does she under estimate, the solemnity of the sudden death ; away in a country parsonage. A priest of God suddenly called into The Presence of God, it is a spectacle that needs no making, it is its own essential drama.

" Rose bent over her husband ; her big plaits swung in his face.

" ' What's the matter, George ? Are you ill ? Are you ill ?' she repeated."

But the sick man is too ill to answer, his world is slipping away from him. A priest must be sent for, in the dead of night, another servant of God must be called.

It is the only thing that now matters from the point of view of the dying man.

" ' Send for Luce.'

" It was the first time he had spoken, and the words jerked out of him dryly without expression."

The reply is so intensely human. The priest must wait, the doctor must be sent for. We always are loath to admit that our loved ones may need a priest, such a procedure looks too much like death. Besides, there is brandy ; it will do the dying person so much good, that brandy in the cupboard, a good strong dose. Of course that terribly stricken figure on the bed is not going to die ; he will be better in the morning ; then the doctor is coming ; absurd to think about sending for a priest.

" Rose was not the sort of woman who could sit still for long—in a moment or two she sprang to her feet and went to the medicine cupboard.

" ' I believe some brandy would do you good—its allowed in case of illness, you know.' "

Cleverly indeed does Miss Kaye-Smith deal with the intense drama. The sick man knows only too well that he is dying ; brandy is no good, a doctor is no good ; only a priest now.

" ' Luce,' he said with difficulty, ' Luce . . . ' "

The scene is not drawn out in the least. We are quickly thrust along to the climax. It is the arrival of the priest. It allows Miss Kaye-Smith to indulge in one of her best pieces of dramatic writing, yet a certain restraint in it, does not produce any unnatural " stage effect."

" Then Rose saw standing behind Gervase, outside the door a tall, stooping figure in a black cloak, under which its arms were folded over something that it carried on its breast."

Miss Kaye-Smith then writes a sentence which I believe to be really great literature, a whole wealth of meaning and profundity in a few words, the sentence that comes perhaps once in a book. Alas so often, a sentence that never comes, much as it might have been wished for.

" The Lord had come suddenly to Leasan Parsonage."

And the coming is frightening, it spells the inevitable failure of the brandy and the doctor. The little bit of bread, the tiny sip of wine, the farewell of one world, the greeting of the next. The muttered words of the priest, the slowly glazing eyes, the shadow of a crucifix. Rose Alard has understood at last.

" She felt someone take her arm and gently pull her aside—the next moment she was unaccountably on her knees and crying as if her heart would break. She saw that the intruder no longer stood framed in the doorway—he was beside the bed, bending over George his shadow thrown monstrous on the ceiling by the candle-light. . . .

" What was he saying. . . . ?

" ' Lord, I am not worthy that thou shouldest come under my roof . . . ' "

.   .   .   .

In all her work, Miss Kaye-Smith shows a certain coldness and aloofness to her characters. Yet this is a strength and not a weakness. A somewhat detached attitude is, I think, quite admirable for a novelist. The novelist can better be a critic, if he adopts a detached air. One of the reasons why Miss Kaye-Smith's characters stand out is that she submits them to a penetrating gaze, a certain amount of disdainful approval ; yet a reasonable amount of sympathy is lavished on them at the same time. She seems to understand their difficulties. Particularly well does she deal with the insoluble problem of class consciousness. This is very well brought out when Miss Jenny Alard is having the difficult experience of falling in love with someone who is in a totally different social position to her. Not easily in rural England do types mix, as far apart as East and West, are the " county" and the farmers. The " county " will hunt over the land of the farmers, but the farmers will only meet the " county " at an annual dinner in the best hotel in the nearest country town.

Miss Alard meets the farmer with whom she is falling in love, and there at once arises in her a very complicated conflict. The surge of love that threatens to overwhelm her is modified by a feeling of something that is almost revulsion, a feeling that she cannot overcome with any ease the traditions of her class. This conflict makes her adopt a cold and haughty manner towards the man she really wants to love. Very significantly does Miss Kaye-Smith deal with this intricate piece of psychology. I think a quotation will show this.

" ' Good-morning Miss Alard. You've come a long way so early.'

" ' Yes, I was coming to Fourhouses—it struck me that you might be willing to sell one of those collie pups you showed me yesterday.' "

Cold and calm words, when the heart is bursting with love, but the lips so often do not convey the emotions of the heart. The heart is not shy, it has no bashfulness, but lips are more reserved, for, to a woman, her lips can never lie, once she has relieved them of any restraint.

" This was not how she had meant to speak. She knew her voice was clipped and cold. Hang it ! she might have managed to break through the wall on this special occasion. First words are the most significant, and she had meant hers to have a more than ordinary warmth, instead of which they had a more than ordinary stiffness."

And there is a very good reason, the curse or blessing, as you wish, of class consciousness, the culture or snobbery, as you wish, of a different bringing up. And a woman is usually far more class conscious than a man. It is easier for a squire to love a shop girl than for the daughter of a squire to love a farmer. If it is asked why this should be so, perhaps it is that a man at times does not look beyond sex, whereas a woman nearly always has wider vision, unless she has become utterly abandoned and has no thought beyond the physical gratification of the moment.

" But it was no good trying—she would never be able so to get rid of the traditions of her class and of her sex as to show this young man that she loved him—if indeed she really did love him."

But a little later, when love has swept aside all worry about tradition, Jenny Alard, in many ways a tiresome superficial character, gives herself utterly. Miss Kaye-Smith records her progress carefully. The climax is admirable ; having got exactly what she wanted, Miss Alard bursts into tears, she is " so silly," she is like so many millions of other silly women, so silly because she wants the kisses of her lover, the physical attractions of his near presence. I do hope Miss Kaye-Smith is not laughing at Miss Alard and her lover from the land, but I rather think she is !

Possibly, in drawing Stella Mount, the girl upon whom so many of the Alard's lavish their affection, Miss Kaye-Smith has given us one of her most attractive characters. The girl is that curious type of person with whom the reader falls earnestly in love. And it probably is because Stella Mount is such a mixture of the child and the sophisticated woman. Her whole life is a conflict ; she desires to be married yet does not marry because she is in love with a man she cannot have. Very poignantly does Miss Kaye-Smith let her express her curious position.

" ' He's keeping me unmarried, and I ought to get married—I don't like spinsters—and I know I was meant to be married.' "

The girl, too, is conscious of a certain weakness, she wants Peter Alard, she wants him in the sense that she

quite obviously desires to possess him. This potential
wish is conveyed to her father in language which indicates
Stella Mount's possession of passion.

" ' I want his love, his kisses, his arms round me.' "

Why ? Because Stella wants physical satisfaction,
because Stella is a full-blooded woman, because Stella is
born to marry, because Stella makes men love her, because
to Stella an enforced virginity is distasteful to her.   But
because of something much more significant than all these
things, yet bound up with them. She expresses the
reason to Dr. Mount.

" ' I want to give . . . oh, father, father.' "

Miss Sheila Kaye-Smith can be defined as a relentless
writer, pursuing her characters, exposing their weaknesses with a grim determination that leaves their very
souls open to a minute inspection. She has no mercy at
times, which is a reason why Miss Kaye-Smith has reached
such a distinguished position in the art she has chosen.
Not very far from the end of the book, when the unfortunate House of Alard is heading towards its inevitable ruin, the author draws a remorseless picture of
Sir John Alard, a picture that is a vivid scrutiny under
which the arrogant and bullying baronet might well quiver,
could he see his own soul placed upon the rack constructed
by a clever and uncompromising writer of fiction.

" Indeed, of late Sir John had grown alarmingly
eccentric. His love of rule had passed beyond the
administration of his estate and showed itself in a
dozen ways of petty dominion. He seemed resolved

to avenge his authority over the three rebellious children on the two who had remained obedient."

The " sympathetic " response to their father proves nothing, for Miss Kaye-Smith so naïvely implies that any excitement might cause poor Sir John to have another stroke. And such an occurrence might be the sudden end of the Alard House.

With an untiring energy Miss Kaye-Smith hurries us along to the climax of the tragedy of the House of Alard. There is the death of the old baronet, then the deplorable suicide of Peter, the social suicide when Jenny marries a farmer.

It is all very sad, this end of an old English family. Miss Kaye-Smith is gloomy and grim, she delights in her own pessimism, she is definitely proud of her occasional bursts into cynicism, perhaps she is not so conscious of how " beautifully " she can write when she chooses.

The two last lines in the book are dire tragedy. There is a pathetic hopelessness about them.

" ' Oh, Father,' sobbed Doris. ' Oh, father—oh, Peter ! . . . What would you have done if you had known how it was going to end ?' "

Miss Kaye-Smith, in my opinion, is one of the cleverest women writers of to-day.

" The End of The House of Alard " seems to me to indicate quite a number of her qualities, her capacity for constructing a tragedy, her ability to write something in one sentence, bringing in, in a few words, an intense drama. Her dialogue seems to indicate a certain aloofness, yet an ardent wish to be accurate in the cause of Realism.

If Miss Kaye-Smith is rather " cruel " to some of her characters, it is because she has a passionate regard for truth. Platitudes creep into her work, but like many platitudes, they are well worth while. Generally speaking, Miss Kaye-Smith is pessimistic, which is a reason why we feel that she will never despair of humanity.

Again, Miss Kaye-Smith has very high powers of writing about love without wallowing in sex or passing it by as though love can be divorced from sex. Her women love, love ; but they like a pound of flesh with it, her men love women both physically and spiritually.

Miss Kaye-Smith has achieved a great deal ; she is a novelist worthy of and in a secure position in the front rank. And perhaps this is so because she is both human and yet a severe critic when she likes, able to be remorseless when such treatment is necessary. In a word, perhaps the best description of her art, is that it is not only art, but very Rational art.

PART TWO
MISS ROSE MACAULAY

MISS ROSE MACAULAY

Elliott & Fry, Lld.

PART TWO

MISS ROSE MACAULAY

In this Essay I propose to concentrate on one book that Miss Macaulay has written. I do not say that it is her best book, it is not even her worst book, it is a book that has a distinct fascination for modern people, in that it is so essentially a modern book. It has all the qualities that constitute modern life ; cleverness, smartness, superficiality, common sense, nonsense. Into " Crewe Train " has Miss Macaulay introduced these varied and yet complementary qualities. For it is one of the marked characteristics of our age, that it is both clever and superficial, overbounding with common sense, full of nonsense, an age that gropes its uneasy way along, an age that has given us a fiction that is a keen reflection of the modern world. Miss Macaulay in " Crewe Train " is intensely modern, and as a corollary, she is smart, clever, superficial, exasperating, without letting any one of these qualities play a too lordly domination. In my examination of this curious and fascinating book I shall hope to show something of Miss Macaulay's elastic mind.

Miss Macaulay has a great talent for putting herself into her characters. So much so, that she may be accused of superficiality, when the correct accusation would be that she was " superficial " because she was writing about a superficial character. She is superficial in the cause of realism, inasmuch as other writers are tragic in the cause of tragedy. When critics write professionally and therefore quite often without caring *very much* what they say, demand that a novelist is superficial, they should realise that realism may quite easily put a novelist in a false position. Yet we cannot blame the professional critics, the newspaper reviewers ; their work is hurried, and they have not the time to delve deeply, so often they accuse a writer of superficiality because modern conditions has made much professional criticism in the newspapers a mere matter of superficial slap dash. I have merely quoted this superficiality question as an example of how the rush of business and many books often lead the purely professional critic into false paths. I am a professional critic, and all the criticism I make is likely to recoil on my own head, but of all people, critics must expect to be severely criticised.

But to return to Miss Macaulay and her novel with the very curious title " Crewe Train." What, of course, the author is writing about, is a girl who is a very peculiar person and a man who is less peculiar. I think I am right if I say that much of the story is about that strange after-the-war commodity, the smart person. You can find smart people in Mayfair who are so smart that they never insist on placarding their smartness ; you can find smart people in Balham who are so smart that in order to let it be known, must cry from the very housetops—we are smart, we play bridge, we don't go to Church, we believe in fifty new religions each ending in an ism, of course we are for divorce, all the best people are, we don't know our neighbours, and of course we all dance the Charleston.

Smart life, we get some of it in " Crewe Train," with a

nice little mixture of Catholicism, about which Miss
Macaulay writes a good deal of silly trash, a great deal
about love, about which Miss Macaulay never writes
anything really silly, and so much about a modern girl,
a curious kind of being. She seems to be rather disagree-
able, or is it that she is wise and prefers her own thoughts
to wasting time talking to foolish and dull people ?

Away out in the lands that are foreign ; it is here that
we find the heroine of the book, Denham Dobie, the girl
about whom Miss Macaulay has written the book I am
attempting to examine. The girl is not sociable !

"Denham Dobie had no intention of giving herself
unnecessary trouble. She evaded even the British
and American tourists whom she did not know, and
who passed from time to time, as they will even in the
Pyrenees, for fear they should ask her the way to somewhere. That was a great nuisance. Denham looking
bored and impassive, would direct them curtly and turn
aside herself in another direction. Why, the devil, she
speculated, couldn't people look out their own ways on
maps ?"

That is the girl that we are to think about, the type of
girl who is not perhaps exactly shy or selfish, but self-
absorbed because she cannot bear contradiction. If we
would follow the easiest path, let us speak to no one, for
then we shall run no risk a sudden smashing of our
ideals. And Denham is an idealist.

Miss Macaulay has one or two trite but true sayings
about the dislike most of us have for meeting tourists
when we are ourselves abroad, in that self same capacity.
This meeting of tourists, so we are informed, spoils the

sense of adventure of foreign travel, because—oh, horrid and sudden end of romance—it reminds us that any one who has a few pounds to spare can travel abroad.

In " Crewe Train " one of the characters puts the matter concisely, he, superior person, being a mere unimportant tourist, cannot bear other tourists. How we hate anything or anybody who breaks up the fond illusion of desperate adventure that we think awaits us, as soon as the dear old white cliffs of Dover have slipped out of sight.

" Partly because it reminds us that, however noble, we, too, are tourists ; partly because it spoils that abroad feeling, and gently speaks of England, home and duty."

I hope I shall not be misunderstood if I say, at times, Miss Macaulay is a " smart " writer. Quick to grasp a bit of inane modern conversation. There's a nice example in a bit of conversation about a cabaret show ; a bit of clever and silly talk about what was seen there. How much leg ; can be implied, how many fat elderly men, with open mouths longing to " *eat* " the long-limbed girls of few brains and no morals.

" Guy came in late, and said next morning that the cabaret had been dull and poor.

" ' The Pyrenees are altogether too primitive. No grace or wit or elegance. I nearly asked for my money back.' "

An admirable picture of the foolish Englishman trying to impress how much he longs for a really scorching show, so that when he gets back to his unobtrusive villa, he can say how much and how far the French really do go. Miss Macaulay brings out an answer to a very direct feminine question, with much cleverness.

" ' What did you see, darling ?' Evelyn asked.
" ' Oh, well it wasn't quite so dull as all that,' said Guy. ' What time is that train ?' "

These last two lines seem to me to indicate to some extent the " smartness " of Miss Macaulay. The direct feminine question parried by the shuffling and indirect masculine reply is indeed typical of much conversation that is indulged in by the sort of sophisticated people about whom Miss Macaulay writes in " Crewe Train."

And in such a piece of dialogue Miss Macaulay is not only " smart," she is also natural. Men may and do go to cabaret shows, which are often the most futile kind of entertainment possible to imagine, but they will not tell their women kind what happened there, quite oblivious of the fact that the average woman longs to know !

In an Essay of this description, dealing with a brilliant modern woman writer, the only way I can hope to do any justice to the theme, is to show how Miss Macaulay deals with certain situations, situations both grave and gay. So I will write what she thinks about Sunday plays in London, at which most of the sophisticated people in London congregate in the hopes of hearing a play that has been considered too nasty for the legitimate theatre.

Miss Macaulay demonstrates for us something of the mind of many dramatists who really do not seem to think that what they write matters a bit, for it is merely for a Sunday play, and the audience will not be particular.

" He meant to write another play for Sundays, more bitter and ironic than ever. And, since it was only for Sundays, he need not be squeamish as to what he said."

. . . .

With a good deal of cunning, Miss Macaulay writes of the headlong way in which so many people, mistaking sex and passion for love, rush into a contract for marriage without any degree of real and sensible consideration. Yet perhaps the essential difficulty is that sex and passion sometimes are love, or at any rate temporary love. The way in which Denham and Arnold are whirled into love is admirably described by Miss Macaulay.

" Both touched the edges of passion as they clung together in the wet yellow evening. They loved to embrace one another ; thrills of joy shivered through them as their lips and hands touched. They were savouring one of the elementary human pleasures."

Not content with writing something extremely rational about her particular two people in " Crewe Train," Miss Macaulay creates a generalisation which has the excellent and uncommon quality of common sense. It is about the undoubted truism that people who are in love do not look ahead. Of course they do not, the dear people don't want to look ahead when their surroundings are heaven, when they are in the ecstasies of reciprocated love. Why, if they looked ahead they might see many horrid and disturbing things—possible loss of affection, certain loss of passionate romance, a transition from a fairy paradise to a commonplace married existence, the changing of the Prince Charming into a mediocre clerk, the elimination of the Fairy Princess into a wife with a dirty apron, and stockings of imitation silk. The only thing that matters when you are in love is the present, the delicious sense of mental and physical satisfaction, the anticipation of an exhilarating climax, the longing for the complete union ; no thought of reaction, disillusion, a sudden fall from dreamland to reality. Miss Macaulay in a few words states her case fairly and with a sympathetic understanding.

" As far as you may, on so slight acquaintance, love, this young man and woman loved now. Neither looked ahead, for to love, to play together and to embrace was, for the time, enough."

The sweet present, with what misery do we often look back to something that is now the past and would with bitter tears demand that the past be the present.

While I am on the subject of love, another example can be quoted, showing how Miss Macaulay deals with the subject. It is the same love compact between Denham and Arnold growing up, but at present by no means grown up ! Before ; we are not quite sure whether the couple were in love or whether they were merely under the hot influence of rapturous kissings, but now Miss Macaulay lets us perceive that it is the real thing, something more solid than passion, a little more stable, but still to be appeased by kisses.

Denham and Arnold are caught by the inevitable, but the inevitable is pleasing.

" By teatime they both perceived that they were in love. The usual kind of strong attraction netted them firmly about, and it would have been of no use to struggle against it, even had they endeavoured to do so.

They knew that they must meet very frequently in London and continue this thing. They made engagements to lunch together this week, to play tennis in Regent's Park and to go to kennel shows. The affair in short promised well."

So much, then, for Miss Macaulay writing about love, she is sympathetic, reasonable, smart and quite nice. I have now to say something about her when she writes about religion, she is not nearly so sensible and is often not quite nice, but religion is the one great theme to bring out the worst in a woman writer. No woman is ever reasonable about religion, it is often for her a substitution for sexual starvation or so firm a belief that mere man has no chance of understanding the attraction it has for her.

In writing about religion Miss Macaulay succeeds in showing quite plainly her limitations. She tries to be clever and flippant and fails, now and again as though by accident she says a reasonable thing or two. But women are never theologians, the Almighty being far too sensible to trust their very doubtful powers of logic !

.　.　.　.　.　.　.　.　.

How ridiculously does Miss Macaulay deal with a certain admonition in the Catholic Catechism which Denham has to study to be eligible for admittance to the Catholic Church. I will give the quotation and then say why in my own opinion Miss Macaulay does not seem to get at the right end of the stick. In fact the stick seems to have turned round and beaten her.

" Denham turned to the end of the Catechism. There was a piece about going to bed, how you must undress modestly, thinking about death. How could one, when

undressing alone, do it modestly or otherwise ? Of
course, one might forget to draw the curtains when the
light was on."

The question of being alone has surely nothing whatever
to do with modesty. And the gibe about drawing the
curtain because the light might be on, is not only cheap and
silly, but offensive. What the Catholic Church means
by the admirable statement about modesty is surely that
the body is something that is Holy for it is the earthly
receptacle of the Soul. To make out that it is something
superficial, as Miss Macaulay does, merely shows that the
author is out of her depths or trying to be witty and smart
with something that has no demand of such treatment.

A little later on Miss Macaulay shows Denham to be a
silly little fool, but even so Miss Macaulay makes her
almost *too* silly about becoming a Catholic. This is a peep
of the " mind " of Denham that we are treated too.

" Oh, yes, she would be a Mohammedan if Arnold
wished it."

However material the motives might be for a change of
religion, I believe it is an exaggeration to embrace Catholicism or Mohammedanism, even at the whim of an ardent
lover.

Yet of course, it has to be conceded in fairness to Miss
Macaulay's book that Denham is intensely stupid. A
line or two suggests this. But what I believe firmly, is
that she is not quite so stupid about Catholicism as Miss
Macaulay would have us think. For she might be, for
the 'sake of her lover, futile in this manner—

" she would eat off as many plates as he liked—hun-

dreds and thousands of plates, and a fresh knife and
fork with each of them "

—but this is a very different thing to being agreeable
to be either a Mohammedan or a Catholic as though such
a change were a mere light nothing.

Again, but a little later, Miss Macaulay writes the most
blatant nonsense when she quietly tells us about Denham
and her coming conversion.

> " She would learn, if necessary, to answer all those
> foolish questions in the Catechism."

I contend very sincerely that no one, however lightly
he regarded a change of religion, would join the Catholic
Church if they thought the Catechism of that Body
" Foolish." They might disagree with it in minor matters,
but that is a totally different thing from thinking the
Catechism Dogmas foolish, and yet joining the Catholic
Church. Miss Macaulay does here, in my opinion, seem
to be writing without any real thought and trying to be
flippant about something that cannot be beaten by that
kind of mediocre satire.

One more quotation with regard to Miss Macaulay's
superficial utterances about Catholicism will suffice. She
makes a rabid Catholic sneer at Anglican parsons in a way
that most Catholics do not employ. Catholics may be " sorry
for " poor misguided Anglican parsons, as they cannot be
" real priests," but they do not usually accuse them of
insincerity. Yet Miss Macaulay writes this absurd piece
of dialogue. It all concerns the question of the necessity
of re-baptism of an Anglican by a Catholic priest.

> " Anglican parsons are so casual," Arnold replied.
> " They don't think it matters."

What on earth is a clever writer like Miss Macaulay thinking about that she should write anything so grossly unfair ? When Miss Macaulay has learnt the fundamentals of Catholicism and something about what the average Anglican clergyman thinks about Baptism, she will possibly save herself from writing nonsense which is exasperating in the extreme.

. . . .

If Miss Macaulay knows nothing about Catholicism she knows a great deal about the foolish kind of wife who has no appreciation of the supreme importance of a review If only wives would realise that to an author, reviews are his most sacred food, if only the good ladies would enthuse even if they do not know what a review really is, if only they would pretend to be sensible when they are merely silly. Authors would then have found Utopia. A delicious piece of conversation is that between Arnold and Denham about a good review, and let it be told to the envious gods, in an important journal.

" A serious weekly periodical said that Mr. Chapel's first novel was one of brilliant promise, and teemed with ideas. It devoted half a column to it, and depreciated another novel in comparison."

And the poor foolish author, burning with the glorious enthusiasm of the review is so unwise as to think that Denham will be equally enthusiastic.

" Arnold read it to Denham at breakfast.
" ' Not bad, is it,' he said.
" ' Very good,' said Denham.
" ' The Weekly Comment review is important of course,' he added.

" ' Is it good ?   Why ?'
" ' Well, because—— Oh, well, it is.   It's read by
people who matter.   It counts.' "

Delicious natural dialogue, but sad, for it is the sign of a
coming catastrophe.   Women seem to have no sense of
tact, they are probably too sincere !

Miss Macaulay has a subtle way of indicating the
evolutionary process which gradually smashes up the
Arnold and Denham marriage.   When a wife is not
enthusiastic about her husband's art, it is a long way
towards the final *dèbacle* of marriage.   Let a wife take no
interest in her husband's work if he is a bank clerk and it
really doesn't matter much ; but let her be indifferent
about her husband when he has the artistic temperament
and she will gradually be ground to powder by his fury.
So Denham is beginning to destroy the marriage.   Miss
Macaulay has stated the first step very skilfully.

And poor Denham, meaning so well, does not get on
very well with those she comes in contact with.   Again
Miss Macaulay brings out this standpoint carefully.

For poor Denham is tongue tied when with other people,
a position that might be created because she was too silly
or too clever to talk to very ordinary and boring people.

" In the friendly, light-hearted circle of Arnold's
friends, with chaff flying brightly from speaker to
speaker, with ridiculous wit alternating with sophisticated discussion or with personal gossip, Arnold's
dark-browed wife would sit silent or monosyllabic."

Another step in the path that is ruining their marriage,
for a brilliant author, a man who is clever enough to write
a novel and get it well reviewed must not have a dull wife.

The author's friends will not have it, the wife must at least be bright enough to be a shadow of her husband's glory. A bank clerk can have, and generally does have, a bank clerk's wife, but an author, an artist, must have the wife fitting for such an exalted personage, and such wives are too rare.

The melancholy result of the whole thing is that people began to think that Arnold's wife " was not quite right in the head." Miss Macaulay writes very knowingly about the way that people regard dull women, at first being angry with them and then with great charity, recognising that the poor things are not *quite* normal, not quite as normal as the normal suburban society which is too dull to attempt to be abnormal !

I rather imagine that Miss Macaulay admires the licence that is allowed in novels in these days. I rather imagine that she thinks nothing need be hid in the very admirable cause of realism. And she is right, nothing should be hid, so long as it makes the artistic presentment of truth more true. Prudes will always object to realism because the real must in many cases be offensive to them. Yet the prude easily shocked and horrified at many of the obscenities of life cannot view life as a whole without at least realising that these obscenities are present.

But when realism is not materially helped, I see no particular merit in reference to matters which, if not coarse, are not at their best in the publicity of cold print.

I am referring to a passage when Miss Macaulay writes with an extreme frankness about poor Denham when she is undergoing the trying process of preparing to have a baby.

" Denham felt, and often was, sick in the mornings."

Really how appallingly dull Miss Macaulay is some-times, as if it is of any interest to know that Denham is very earnestly sick in the cause of having a baby. After all some thousands of women are daily sick in the good cause, but the matter is merely one of discomfort to the person concerned.

I will conclude my survey of some of the aspects of Miss Macaulay with a quotation about the dear old subject of love.

Thus she writes with all the dogmatism that women use when they write about love.

" Love's a disease. But curable. It passes."

But Miss Macaulay's dogmatism is seriously at fault. Love is never a disease, it is a God-given gift, it is never curable, it never passes except when lust is mistaken for love.

. . . .

Miss Macaulay is a very peculiar kind of novelist. She can and does at times write brilliantly, yet now and again she falls into the banal. Her greatest fault is a certain superficial flippancy, especially about the matters of reli-gion, to which some reference has been made. She has great powers of " smart " writing and perhaps this is her most outstanding characteristic. Her characters, gene-rally speaking, seem to be natural, though perhaps Miss Macaulay is a little liable to exaggeration in an attempt to make the characteristics of her characters outstanding. Her realism is tinged with an obvious pandering to the disgusting licence that certain women novelists take such a pernicious delight in exhibiting.

Miss Macaulay is more clever than charming or perhaps

it is, that she is too clever or not clever enough to be charming. Using the word in the popular and therefore most easily understood application, Miss Macaulay is " interesting."

Perhaps Miss Macaulay is clever and therefore rather inclined to be superficial, perhaps she is flippant without realising that flippancy has no effect on serious matters, perhaps Miss Macaulay is a strange contradiction a smart novelist and at times a very shallow thinker.

But Miss Macaulay is a modern woman writer, she could not under the circumstances be expected to avoid a certain shallowness. She seems to be characteristic of her type, the woman novelist who must write modern books, mention that women are sick before they have babies. It is a type that will die out when modern woman, having travelled in a vicious circle, comes back to realise that modernism in literature and fiction is but a reaction from the standpoint of the last century.

PART THREE
MISS ETHEL M. DELL

PART THREE

MISS ETHEL M. DELL

THERE is no writer of to-day who is more widely read than Miss Dell. To produce a novel that runs into nearly fifty editions is a remarkable achievement even in this century when nothing is remarkable ! And the curious part of the whole thing is that superior people rather laugh at Miss Dell, but the laugh has more than a suggestion of malice behind it and not a little perplexity. In this Essay I am going to make an attempt by an examination of something of the art of Miss Dell to give some idea of why she is so popular. And let me say at the very outset that I believe Miss Dell thoroughly deserves her popularity. And she deserves it because she has made her art " something " which has in the strict sense discovered that mysterious entity that we call the general public. In my examination of some of the aspects of Miss Dell, I have confined myself to her best known book—" The Way of an Eagle."

. . . .

There is undoubtedly a very wide class of people who are delighted when they come across a novelist whose work requires no special effort to read. Miss Dell is the kind of novelist who can be read when the mind is too tired to undertake any intricate process of thinking, when a problem novel would be a misery, when an intricate character study would merely bore and annoy. Miss Dell makes but one conscious effort with her art, she is out with the whole strength of her being, to create something that is entertaining.

There are a vast number of people who want nothing better than to spend an evening with Miss Dell, or they like her to accompany them on the wholly detestable daily journey from the suburbs. Whether this taste is a commendable one, is a matter of personal opinion. I do not believe that such a taste is as deplorable as some of our professional critics would suggest. For whatever may be said against Miss Dell on the grounds that she writes cheap melodrama and of love of the scullery type, her books in the best sense are clean, and it is an excellent thing that clean books should find so wide a public. But so many modern people, especially those who are intellectual, have no hatred of fiction dirt so long as it is reasonably clever.

If a very large number of people did not lead unromantic and unexciting lives, perhaps Miss Dell would not be so popular. Miss Dell is rather like a general store, she supplies something that many people lack. She supplies the kind of life that is romantic even if this romance is exaggerated and only to be found in books. Many people base their delicious dreams on what they read in books, on what they find between the covers of a novel. Miss Dell creates dream people, by which I mean that she creates people who have their abode in that imaginary world of romance that the degrading *thrust* of daily life can seldom entirely eliminate.

The intellectuals sneer at Miss Dell because the intellectuals have long lost the secret of life. The secret of life has eluded the sophisticated machines that our universities turn out, but it has been revealed to the servant girl who sits in her dark kitchen and revels in the gamut of love that oozes out of Miss Dell's books.

For the essence of Miss Dell is her writing about love. The whole attraction of her writing centres round this passionate emotion. Of course, Miss Dell is not deep, she is far too popular to be so ! She has her very well defined limitations, and did she lose them, she would probably lose a greater part of her public. There is, in her writing, something childlike, which is precisely the opposite from saying that it is in any way childish. The world always really craves for that which is childlike, while it detests that which is childish. The childlike writer has an art that is built on an eternal, the childish writer has an art that is built on very shifting sand. Miss Dell is, in certain aspects, a childlike writer, she is never, as far as I judge, childish.

The difference is stupendous, yet many critics have entirely failed to see the difference. But critics are never childlike ; quite often they are merely childish ! You may laugh at Miss Dell, you may sneer at her simplicity, but deep down you will know you have laughed because you are far too sophisticated and successful to cry.

Miss Dell is simple, but she is never silly. Now and again she makes a very slight attempt to philosophise, and then her philosophy seems to be based on common sense. Sometimes she comments on a course of action, but, unlike many novelists, her novels never develop into being mere commentaries, just to show us how fiction can be stretched, until it becomes merely the philosophy of the novelist who happens to be writing.

It is a platitude to say so (but platitudes are invariably

worth considering), that Miss Dell writes a good story whereas many novelists write very bad stories. Having attempted to state a few generalisations concerning Miss Dell, it will be perhaps interesting to show exactly how she does deal with various events, by means of a discussion of her book, " The Way of an Eagle." And let it be said that it is no small achievement to have written such a book and made it appeal to so many thousands of those curious mysteries, whom we label, knowing the term to be utterly contradictory and a libel—ordinary.

.   .   .   .

In " The Way of an Eagle " we are shown the type of man that most men hate and many women love. The type of man who is always unboundedly conceited, withal nearly a bounder, eternally cheerful, always in love with some woman and always, always, always whistling when things look most black. In other words, a stage hero, a cool imperturbable kind of creature who is never at a loss for some appropriate action or some appropriate reply.

Whether Miss Dell's characters are exaggerated is a matter of opinion, but the problem has no effect on the story, and therefore can be severely left to those who are never tired of all kinds of literary puzzles. Suffice it to say that, exaggerated or not, her characters have a certain attraction about them. Even if the attractiveness is the attractiveness of polished insolence, feminine superficiality, and English snobbery of the most arrogant nature.

Miss Dell has a great power of writing melodrama in a few words. There is a good instance of this when Nick Ratcliffe and Muriel Roscoe are flying from the fort which has been taken by the Blacks. We are to imagine there has been the thick darkness of a tropic night.ˈ Then, suddenly Nick speaks :

" ' See,' he said.   ' Here comes the dawn.' "

Intense melodrama in a few words, the coming of the dawn—with what joy we behold the dawn when we have been awake all night ; it is with the dawn that so many start for their last journey ; it is with the dawn that so many are born into this world; so often at sea, it is with the coming of the dawn that we behold a new land.   The dawn, the end of the night and the beginning of the new day, the transition from thick and unreasoning darkness to the glimmer of the coming daylight.   Miss Dell announces with all her sense of the dramatic, the coming of day.   Perhaps this keen and constant sense of the dramatic is a characteristic of Miss Dell.

Again, in my attempted discovery of the reason of the immense popularity of Miss Dell, I believe that this sense of the dramatic plays no small part.   The sense of the dramatic not only grips the reader, it pilots him along, allows his emotions to follow a normal course, prepares him for more drama and yet does not allow him to wallow in something that can so easily become cheap melodrama.

I will give another example of how Miss Dell suddenly jumps from a scene of peace to a scene of terror.   Muriel Roscoe, under the influence of a swiftly running stream :

" Under its soothing influence she might have slept, a blessed drowsiness was stealing over her,"—

And then Miss Dell prepares the reader for a swift change of atmosphere—

" when suddenly there flashed through her being a swift warning of approaching danger."

The transition from one emotion to another is here most skilfully conceived.

It creates a feeling of lively anticipation in the reader. In fact, I contend that all Miss Dell's work has this merit.

Miss Dell evidently has a great belief in the undoubted fact that a great many women like being ordered about by a man. And especially when the man is of the type of Nick Ratcliffe.

A few lines of dialogue between Nick and Muriel will indicate what I mean.

" ' Oh, go away ! Go away !' she wailed. ' Let me die ! '

" ' I will go away,' he answered, swiftly, ' if you will promise to drink what is in this cup.'

" He pressed it against her hand, and she took it almost mechanically. ' It's only brandy and water,' he said. ' You will drink it ? ' "

Then we have the spectacle of the woman absolutely obeying the man, and feminism may be utterly outraged— Miss Dell's women seem to rather like the process of obeying.

" ' If I must,' she answered weakly.
" ' You must,' he rejoined."

Yet again Miss Dell deals quite sincerely with life at bedrock, life stripped of all the inane conventionalities which society has heaped upon it, life face to face with nature, life desperately struggling, life, when the spirit of it refuses to be beaten. There is a fine piece of naked human nature when bread is scarce and the appetite demands, with no shadowed insistence, that it must be appeased and appeased at once.

There is no opportunity for any kind of convention when starvation or the threat of it hovers in the vicinity.

> " ' You are to eat it,' she said very decidedly. ' You shall eat it. Do you hear, Nick ? I know what is the matter with you. You are starving. I ought to have seen it before.' "

This time it is the woman who orders. It is the man who obeys. Something of the situation so common to that brilliant writer, Mr. Jack London. Miss Dell brings out something that I might call the innate fineness of humanity. So many of our present day novelists, excellent as they are as artists, only depict humanity as trivial, second rate, without any sterling qualities, lust laden, overawed by sex. But Miss Dell makes her characters grapple with very appalling situations, and for the most part she makes them come out well.

In the case of Nick Ratcliffe, though he is almost a bounder at times, a certain unselfishness saves him from such a fate. He puts himself last, while so many present day novelists create characters who always put themselves first. There is no need to ask which class of character is most popular with the novel reading public. Miss Dell is the answer !

If Miss Dell has powers of the dramatic sense, she has also considerable powers of creating the background for drama, the background that describes to the reader by means of really great word pictures. Perhaps one of the

best of these is when Nick, nearly at the end of his re-
sources, gazes over the unemotional mountains, those
mountains which show no emotion because they are
eternal.

" All through the long, burning hours he never
stirred away from her.   He sat close to her, often holding her in his arms, for she seemed less restless so ; and
perpetually he gazed out with terrible, bloodshot eyes
over the savage mountains, through the long, irregular
line of pass, watching eagle-like, tireless and intent, for
the deliverance, which, if it came at all, must come that
way.   As the sun sank in a splendour that transfigured
the eternally white mountain-crest to a mighty shimmer
of rose and gold he turned at last and looked down at the
white face pillowed upon his arm."

Though perhaps the actual situation may be one that is
open to question on the grounds of realism, there can be
no doubt that this is a finely-written piece of description,
not overdrawn, with just that touch of delicate romance
which Miss Dell never leaves very far in the background.
For though the mountains are savage, though the pass is
relentless, though exhaustion is tearing a man and a girl
to shreds, there is the faint light of love, the sense of
chivalry.   And in the far distance come the horses and the
chariots, as in the old days when God led His armies,
when the world was very young.   The girl very nearly
dead—Miss Dell writes of her confusion of mind admirably.

" ' Don't you remember how it went ?' " And
behold—the mountain—was   full—of   horses—and
chariots—of—fire !"   God sent them, you know.' "

.   .   .   .

It is quite extraordinary how sometimes Miss Dell falls into trivial inanities. When Muriel suddenly decides after all that she will not marry Nick, Miss Dell makes her state her momentous decision in the feeble trash that has made so many think that Miss Dell can only write trash.

" ' Yes, I am silly,' she acknowledged. ' I'm perfectly idiotic to fancy for a moment that it can make any difference to you. Nick, I have been thinking things over seriously, and—and—I find that I can't marry you after all.' "

All this is absolutely untrue to life ; surely no reasonable woman talks like this ; and also when Muriel descends to these depths of banality, I believe that Miss Dell is making Muriel quite inconsistent with herself. It is in a passage like this that we see Miss Dell writing exaggerated nonsense, and many critics of her work have condemned her entire work because of these pitiable lapses.

How extremely different is the power of Miss Dell but a little later. When there is that strangest of all tragedies, the death of a very young child, a little life that is swept away almost before it had been conscious that it was alive. In this part of her work Miss Dell again writes excellent drama and avoids exaggerated melodrama.

Into this scene, with considerable sympathy and tact, Miss Dell combines pathos and drama, violent grief and the cold relentlessness of premature death. Death has swooped down, with a callous disregard which is his birthright, he has " delighted " in snatching a child away into the Unknown.

" Jim Ratcliffe was silent for a moment while he

gazed at the little lifeless form he held. Then very
gently, very pitifully, but withal very steadily, his
verdict fell through the silent room.

" ' He will never cry any more.' "

It is again the acme of drama in a few well chosen words.
A reply to the grief stricken mother is a very excellent
piece of psychology.

" Quietly he drew the head-covering over the baby's
face. ' My dear,' he said, ' there is no death.' "

When death has just done his worst, when the body is
still quite warm when, the heart has only just ceased to
beat ; it is then that people will listen to the assertion that
there is no such thing as death. Death is the one event
that convinces that there is no actual reality in death,
for were death the end, there would be no *grief* over the
cold body, but madness, suicide, for the end would not be
temporary, but endless and inevitable. It is only when
we gaze at a dead body, that we know there is no death
but a physical ending to generate a spiritual beginning.
And it is this beginning which the Materialists ignore
which makes their position so untenable directly we are
brought face to face with Physical death. Miss Dell has
written a truism and an admirable piece of realism.

I have already said that Miss Dell is a fine descriptive
artist when the scene is savage and unrestrained. She has
equal skill in writing of the exquisite peace and charm of
an Eastern night. There is a pleasing sense of brooding
about the description.

" A gorgeous sunset lay in dusky, fading crimson
upon the Plains, trailing to darkness in the east. The
day had been hot and cloudless, but a faint, chill wind
had sprung up with the passing of the sun, and it flitted

hither and thither like a wandering spirit over the
darkening earth. Down in the native quarter a tom-
tom throbbed, persistent, exasperating as the voice of
conscience. Somewhere in the distance a dog barked
restlessly at irregular intervals. And at a point between
tom-tom and dog a couple of parrots screeched voci-
ferously. Over all the vast Indian night was rushing
down on silent, mysterious wings."

There is no attempted stage play about this, the mysterious Eastern night is reasonably conveyed.

In this description there may be found a certain quality
which is seldom attributed to Miss Dell. That is a certain atmosphere of melancholy, the quiet grave and kindly
sympathy of the night, the kindly peace that the night
brings with her, the motherly care with which she sends
tired humanity to sleep. Miss Dell conveys a good deal
of this atmosphere at times.

At the end of " The Way of an Eagle " Miss Dell writes
of that subtle something that all lovers feel when the
magic and ecstatic spell of love has intoxicated them with
the delirious chains which bind them. It may be a sentimental ending to a book, it may be slightly " treacly,"
it may be entirely unintellectual, but it is a beautiful
ending, and so beautiful that sophisticated people will be
left sadly wondering *why* the beautiful is so simple and so
commonplace. And if they think a little deeper they will
realise that the beautiful is always simple, which is why
love which is simple and not vilely intellectual always
baffles those who would interpret the emotion in terms of
reason and mathematical decision.

I believe in the passage that I quote, Miss Dell manages
to blend simplicity and beauty admirably together.

" Later, hand in hand, they looked across the valley to the shining crags that glistened spear-like in the sun.

" A great silence lay around them—a peace unspeakable—that those silver crests lifted into the splendour of Infinity.

" They stood alone together—above the world—with their faces to the mountains.

" And thus standing with the woman he loved, Nick spoke, briefly—it seemed lightly—yet with a certain tremor in his voice.

" ' Horses,' he said, ' and chariots—of fire !' "

And perhaps, in imagination, so many thousands of Miss Dell's readers stand and see in the far distance those mountains, those horses, those chariots, burning with unquenchable fire—so that the flames light up the sordid scene of reality and transpose it into the wake of the plunging gleaming cohorts of chariots and horses and fire !

. . . .

In what, then, does the secret of Miss Dell's popularity lie ? I believe first and foremost the answer is that she can write a love story which is entirely removed from anything sordid or even problematical. I believe Miss Dell creates for many thousands of people a romance, that they may have in their own minds, but are quite unable to express. We are all romantic at heart until the world or the people in it have driven it away. Those who sneer at Miss Dell, and they are many, would be well advised to pause and consider whether they have, after all, made much of life. Miss Dell is not in any sense a profound writer, yet her simplicity quite often perplexes those who would claim to be profound.

A very keen sense of the dramatic gives Miss Dell the

impetus to carry off situations that often border on the mere sentimental. Now and again she falls to the most amazing banality, the more amazing when she can rise to real artistic heights.

It would be absurd to claim for Miss Dell any real " literary " qualities, to use that much abused and difficult word. As a novelist, critics who will be so superficial as to use the odious method of critical comparison will be unable to place Miss Dell at all satisfactorily. Miss Dell cannot be placed with other novelists, she has her own place. And that place is a very firm one in the hearts of many thousands of those people we term the mass public.

Miss Dell writes a " pure " story and the story is purely a tale ! The general novel reader likes to read of love, strong men, women who like strong men ; the general reader therefore likes to read Miss Dell. Educated people, intellectual highbrows, sophisticated professional critics, do not like to read Miss Dell. She is too clever for them, and these superior people will not admit that they have been badly hoodwinked.

The world is dark, the area steps look grimy, the clock ticks monotonously on the mantelpiece. But Miss Dell brings romance to the kitchen, romance to the underlings of life. The intellectuals pass her by with a haughty disdain ; it is their intention to turn to the novelists who write so admirably of divorce, materialism, pessimism, adultery and all the things that interest smart people.

But Miss Dell keeps to the heights of simple clean love. She gives romance to those who are most receptive. And I believe that much of Miss Dell's work is as valuable as that of many a novelist about whom the professional critics are so wildly enthusiastic.

PART FOUR
THE BARONESS ORCZY

THE BARONESS ORCZY

Elliott & Fry, Ltd.

PART FOUR

THE BARONESS ORCZY

I SUPPOSE even the most uncritical reader would notice on reading the work of the Baroness Orczy, that there was established between the reader and the writer, a pleasant intimacy. I mean that the Baroness takes the reader into her confidence and writes for him, as though the communication was by word of mouth, rather than by the necessarily more formal written word. This intimacy can be found very largely in the book that I am examining in this Essay, the book that is probably the Baroness at the height of her art, that brilliant mixture of a tale and the study of a people, the book that has the dramatic title of " A Son of the People."

On the very first page of this particular book, I find a good instance of the intimacy I have already suggested. It is almost as if the author was engaging in the easy intimacy of an armchair conversation.

The pleasant question, the frank admission, the sudden remembrance almost, that it is not a conversation, but a description conveyed by the pen, the love of the lovely country of Hungary, all so harmoniously conveyed by the Baroness Orczy.

" Do you love the mountains, English reader—the

romantic peaks of the Rhine country, the poetic heights of the Alps, the more gently undulating slopes of your own South Downs ?"

There, then, is the agreeable wish on the part of the author, that the Englishman shall love his own country, the beauties that his own land can provide—and then the author expresses her own delights, her absorbing passion for the mysterious and glorious country that lies by the Danube.

" As for me, I must confess to an absorbing, a passionate fondness for the lowlands, the wild mysterious plains of Hungary, that lie, deep down, between the Danube and the Theisz, and whenever I stand on those vast pusztas, it always seems to me that the mind must be more free, when the gaze can travel untrammeled to that far-distant horizon which fancy can people at its own sweet will."

As though it were unkind to leave us, who have not travelled to Hungary, unsatisfied with what it is that so delights our author, the Baroness Orczy paints in her own inimitable language what meets the eye in that great and magic country. For our author is a kindly soul, and would have us know that which perhaps so many of us will never see.

" See, how far away that horizon seems, there, where the earth and sky meet in a soft-tones line of purple the merging of the blue sky with the ruddy, sandy soil of the earth. The air trembles with the intense heat, and as the eye tries to define what lies beyond that mysterious vastness, lo ! there suddenly rises on the distant horizon, a vision of towers, minarets, and steeples, white and cool looking, mirrored in some fairy pond that must lie somewhere."

Surely a beautiful description, indicating that sense of awe and wonder which strikes the beholder of a vast view, when the end of that view is in an indescribable nothingness, and yet a nothingness which holds immense possibilities.

This sense of the greatness of a nothingness grips the Baroness as something that is almost human, in that we can so intensely love it. For the marvel of a great view is that it is at once personal and impersonal, personal as the expression of the Mind of God, impersonal as something that cannot be explained by reason, something that is limitless, something that speaks of a world to come, that will be more vast, more inscrutable, yet even more beautiful than our view, for it will be a nearer approach to Heaven.

" Far, very far away, a windmill stretches out its long wings, like a gigantic bird of prey, and right across the plain, the high road, riddled with ruts, wanders northwards, towards Kecskemet."

That is all, and then the almost bitter climax, when space transcends sight, and all is a vast vastness.

" And that is all ! Nothing more. Only sky and earth, and vastness—immeasurable vastness—all one's own : to grasp, to understand, to love !"

. . . .

All through " A Son of the People " we are face to face with the strange and fascinating problem of a superstitious peasantry and the advent of new machinery. The march of Science has ever been coupled with the tumultuous shouts of a troubled people. For a people which is not highly intelligent does not realise that a fight against the coming of machinery is a mere waste of time, it likewise fails to realise that in the end machinery will help, even if it inflicts hardship and unemployment temporarily. The Baroness Orczy deals with this problem carefully and sympathetically in the book I am discussing ; we get an admirable insight into the hatred of the coming machinery and the superstitious peasantry who see in its workings the hand of Satan. One of the peasants expresses the thought very clearly.

" ' The lord of Bideskut has made a compact with the devil,' thundered the giant. ' How do we know that, when our bodies are starved to death, he has not arranged to deliver our souls to his friend Satan ?' "

It is that curious idea that seems to exist among the peasant classes, that the overlord has not only powers over their bodies but also powers over their soul. It is perhaps fortunate that an inaccuracy exists with regard to the latter contention ! It is also curious that countries that are superstitious also try to neutralize certain superstitions by distinct and picturesque Catholic ceremonies and rites. Thus, after the contention of the " handing over " to Satan, we have another peasant demanding the neutralising or thwarting influence of the Mass.

" ' I am for asking Pater Ambrosius to say a special Mass, to keep the devil away,' suggested a young herdsman at last."

And only a little later, when the coming machinery has been forgotten, we have a glimpse of the dear fairy-like picturesqueness of the peasantry, their sudden falling into a form of childlike play, a glimpse given so exquisitely by the Baroness Orczy, so delicately, so naïvely.

" And with true Hungarian light-heartedness, the swarthy giant, forgetting the devil and his works, the lord of Bideskut and his steam mills, proceeded with a merry laugh to chase the pretty woman round the table ; while the young herdsmen delighted with the scene—which was much more in accordance with their lazy sunny dispositions than talks of devil or plots against my lord."

There is that which is very healthy about this description somehow making us believe that there may be something inhuman about machinery and something quite innocent and Divine about humanity when it is in the grip of boisterous play.

Another difficult problem that is contained in " A Son of the People " is that which concerns the overpowering hatred and contempt for the Jews. It is true that the Baroness Orczy makes the Jewish moneylender an unscrupulous blackguard, at the same time she quite fairly shows in all its hideous bareness the attitude of the peasantry to the Jews. Treated worse than dirt, thrown here and there, what virtue can be expected to be fostered by such vile treatment ? If the Jew in Hungary is vile, it is the Hungarian who has made him so.

It is much the same in England. The Englishman with his expressed opinion that he is the most elect being in the Universe, sneers at the Jew, makes the most inane jokes about his characteristics, looks down upon him, while admitting that he is " deuced clever," and then turns round and grumbles because the Jew has but little virtue, when the Englishman has already implied that he has none !

The Baroness Orczy tries very sincerely to show the point of the view of the Jew and the point of view of the non-Jew. It is disquieting reading, for no reading is more disquieting than that which demonstrates the utter inhumanity that humanity can show, and does show, to humanity. In such a case as the hatred of the Jews, humanity is a more deadly menace than machinery, and much more Satanic. By means of several quotations I shall hope to show how the Baroness Orczy deals with the Jewish question in " A Son of the People." She deals with the problem much more faithfully than does Mr. Belloc, whose persistent childishness in some matters in relation to that people, is positively incredible.

A little bit of description of the aristocratic disdain for the Jew is well brought out when the Jewish money-lender Rosenstein attempts to pay an obsequious saluta-tion to the Countess Irma.

" The next moment the Jew, with doubled spine and obsequious bow, entered humbly into the room. As the Countess sailed majestically past him, he tried to stoop still lower, and to kiss the hem of her gown, but gathering her skirts closely round her, and without vouchsafing him the merest look, she left her husband alone with him."

There is a striking parallel to the contempt that the modern world in many respects has for the Palestinian Jew, who has been clever enough to let no one really know exactly what he was. It is a little alarming to reflect that contempt of the Jews is contempt of the Christ, and if the Church is correct, contempt of God. For we rather forget that the Christian God was a Jew, though no doubt this was a Divine mistake and the " nationality " of Christ should have been English !

If there is violent reciprocated hatred on the part of the Jews for the Hungarian aristocracy, there is indeed good reason for this hatred. The Baroness Orczy does not shield the Hungarians ; her frankness is very commendable, and depicts the passionate love for truth which characterises all her writings. The feelings of revenge for centuries of oppression begin to smoulder ominously in the breast of the Jewish moneylender. How terribly true it is that even a worm will turn, yet how much more devastatingly untrue is it to suggest that the Jew is a worm.

" The Jew paused awhile, and looked up one instant at the aristocratic figure before him. Tall and powerful, with proud-looking eyes and noble bearing, Bideskut stood as the very personification of the race which for centuries had buffeted, tormented, oppressed the Jews, denying them every human right, treating them worse than any dog or gipsy."

Then comes the interesting question ! A people may accept tyranny for a long period of time, but the time for revenge comes slowly but surely, and the more slowly the more terrible is it when it comes. The French Revolution, Bolshevism in Russia to-day—who dares to say that these calamities have not been forced by tyranny and autocracy ?

" Was the worm turning at the latter half of the nineteenth century ? Would the oppressed, armed with their patiently massed wealth, turn on the squandering, improvident oppressor, secure in the gold, which very soon would rule even this fair Arcadia, the Hungarian lowlands ?"

God help a people when the worm turns, for it will never turn back until it has gnawed and devastated the very vitals of the people it is determined to destroy.

But the Jew is not to have his revenge as yet ; he is to be made the sport of all those who throng a great nobleman's kitchen ; he shall be made to disobey his most sacred religious orders ; he shall be made to eat an accursed unclean thing ; but the laughter will be turned to weeping, and those who joke will find that the joke is more lengthy than they had imagined. Baroness Orczy gives a magnificent picture of the unfortunate Jewish moneylender swallowing pork, and only swallowing it lest he be outrageously choked.

" In the meanwhile Benko had carved two magnificent slices of meat, and with much laughter, the two men were gradually forcing the Jew to put one piece after another into his mouth. He tried to struggle, but in vain, his tormentors had a very tight hold of him, and when he made futile efforts not to swallow the morsels forbidden by the laws of his race, they held his mouth and nose in a tight grip, so that he was forced to swallow lest he should choke."

There is humour in this description, but also a profound melancholy, for laughter at religious beliefs, however absurd and ludicrous they may appear to the nonbeliever, is never really funny. When we laugh at a belief we exhibit the shocking spectacle of crass superficial merriment. It is only the ignorant who can afford to laugh at a religious belief, or those who are too intellectual to be able to believe anything.

We have the sombre picture of the outraged Jew dismissed after his odious meal. It is rather a terrible picture, for silent unfathomable malice is a dreadful condition, destroying to the body and of deadly insult to the soul. The Jewish moneylender is convulsed with an inward passion, something so terrible that it cannot be easily expressed.

There is no exaggeration in the word picture painted by the Baroness Orczy. It is terrible it is uncompromising, it is deadly, it is as human nature at present is—inevitable.

" For full five minutes Rosenstein the Jew stood at the gates, his thin hands clutching the iron fretwork, his colourless eyes aglow with inward passion, the very personification, the living statue, of a deadly revengeful hatred. For full five minutes he stood there, till he saw a graceful vision in white come wandering down the sweet-scented alley, then he once more turned towards the village, and went his way."

How appalling is the contrast between the sweet countryside and the devouring hatred than can turn humanity into a roaring beast, eager to tear humanity to pieces, demanding to be satiated with full flowing blood, caring save for only one thing, revenge sure and full. Well may the gods weep that mankind made in their image can so distort that image that it becomes almost unrecognizable.

The undying hatred between man and man that is so prominently displayed in " A Son of the People " is sombre reading. And it is possibly the more sombre in that Hungary is a professing religious country, crossed with the Sign of the Cross, fed on the Blessings of the Mass, a witness to the Everlasting Church, yet treating an outcast Jewry with diabolical contempt and tyrannical bullying. The contrast of the human mind is too great for man to understand, the parallel of Religious Observance and inhuman treatment of other people, too puzzling.

　·　　·　　·　　·　　·　　·　　·　　·

The Baroness Orczy just touches upon an unpleasing subject, a subject which we do not care to hear much about, for we know that it is only too true ! That is, the dislike that foreigners have for England. The Hungarian nobleman voices that dislike in no small measured tones. Perhaps if there is one reason above all others why the English are disliked it is to be found in their execrable manners and deplorable assumption when in foreign countries.

" ' Hey ! do not talk to me about that accursed country. What do I know about it, except that it is near the sea, that their corn is coarser than that which we give to the pigs, and that they make wine out of gooseberries ? I ask you what can they know about corn, or about grapes ? ' "

After all, this does little more than indicate the disdain that the foreigner has for the foreigner ; his refusal to admit that he does not know best about everything. One day, when every nation has had a chance of learning something about every other nation, we may get some chance of international understanding. For my part, I believe the first and the most important step is the interchange of books between country and country, race and race. Where missionaries seem to have failed in certain directions books may quite conceivably win. As an example, a " mere novel " it is that I am examining, but when we have read it we have quite a beginning of wisdom about the Hungarians, their likes, their superstitions, their feastings, their revenges.

I will turn to that most charming part of " A Son of the People," the method by which the Baroness Orczy depicts something of the love passion of the Hungarian people. It is grand and primitive, emotional in an artistic sense, rigidly exclusive, class conscious in the extreme.

There is a horrible reality between Ilonka's dream of love and her awakening to the bitter facts of a worldly mother and a worldly outlook. The Baroness Orczy contrasts the two situations with no little skill. Here is Ilonka dreaming of love, giving herself up to delicious imaginings, immersed in the sea of fantastic passion.

> "All day she dreamt of what she so little understood : of a man's passion, of marriage, and blissful life with one whom it was paradise even to listen to, when he whispered so often, and oh ! so ardently, ' I love you, Ilonka !' "

And then the cold relentless reality, the deplorable dialogue with her mother, the shattering of a dream, how hatefully true it all is. The commercial side of love, a good marriage, a sound income, prosperity and respectability, no clandestine meetings, no burning passion, a business contract.

"'I came to tell you, Ilonka, that I was extremely displeased with you,' she began drily.

"'With, me Mama?'

"'Your conduct with that penniless Madach is positively indecent.'

"'Oh, Mama!'

"'Everyone remarked on it to-night. I assure you I blushed for you the whole evening.'

"'Mama!'"

And so her mother easily smashes the dream. It is all so well brought out.

"When her mother finally left her after half-an-hour's steady preaching on children's obedience and maidenly reserve, the poor little girl threw herself on the bed in a passionate flood of tears."

And here is the bitter climax.

"Ilonka cried till she fell asleep, and in her sleep once more dreamt such dreams that made her forget the realities, her stern mama, the midnight lecture, and once more brought, floating before her mind, visions of a handsome young face, with a pair of dark eyes, which, somehow, always made her blush when they met her own, and to her ear the softly whispered words sweeter than song of birds or chorus of angels: 'I love you, Ilonka!'"

It is rather sad all this, for silly careless mothers take a delight in breaking hearts all the wide world over, and so many tears are caused that, were they to be poured into the seas, the seas would run over.

But we must proceed from love to that which is dreadfully prosaic, that which has so much to do with " A Son of the People "—one of the blessings and curses of civilisation—machinery. For machinery is a blessing in that it spells comfort to those who hate a natural life, but it is curse because machinery so often makes human machines, that men and women may be fat and rich and unrestrainedly vulgar.

But in Baroness Orczy's book the fear of the machinery is that it will rob the peasant of his work, his family of their bread, that it will shatter his little home, that it will bring misery and desolation and make of no use the human worker.

" ' Do you see those stacks, Andras,' said one of the men ; ' that wheat is to be threshed and ground into flour, all within a day, and never the hand of thresher or miller is to touch it.' "

The menace of speed ; for machinery can do in one hour that which many men could not do in a day. Yet the fight against machinery is such a hopeless one, you cannot kill Science even if you bring out knives and revolution to aid the warfare. It is almost as hopeless as expecting to kill a Religion by executing or murdering its Chief Priest.

The extreme deference of the peasant for the overlord is clearly indicated by Baroness Orczy when she describes Andras visiting Bideskut to warn him that the populace will not put up with his imported threshing machinery.

There is no meeting ground between lord and peasant in Hungary.

" The long taught deference of the peasant for the

noble induced him to avoid the main entrance and noble staircase."

Not very long after the interview we are introduced to a horrid thing. Listen ! What is that dull murmur ? What is that indefinable hatred ? Why are those knives being sharpened ? What is that thin ominous curl of smoke far away across the plains ? Why do men and women talk so earnestly together ? Why is the lord in his castle looking at the wall to see if there be writing upon it ? Listen again—that slow measured tread ; listen yet again—death is appearing just out of the mists. Why are the great houses barricaded ? It is the beginning of a revolution. The turning of the worms ; the revolt of the people against the aristocratic tyranny ; the revolt of men and women against the deadly danger of machinery. How wonderfully does the Baroness Orczy indicate the beginning of a revolution.

" ' Forgive me, my lord, if I interrupt. It is that mill which is causing so much trouble. It has raised great fears in the minds of the women ; the men themselves, though they will not admit their terror, curse under their breath the contrivance which will take the bread out of their mouth, for want of sufficient wage.' "

The vague threat, the feeling of fear, they are the warnings of a coming revolution.

. . . .

It is again a very long way from these ominous threats to the pleasant light conversation between two lovers. It is the Baroness Orczy at the other extreme of her art—almost a " playful " way of writing.

" ' Rerzso, you know I have forbidden you to kiss me,' she said with a frown.

" ' That is why I like to do it, my soul. What fun would there be in kissing the girls, if they would let you ?' "

Shortly after this pleasing interlude the Baroness Orczy becomes serious again, and she writes some extremely sane remarks on the peasantry who belong to the Church but do not understand it.

It is that curious state of mind which is perfectly content to rely on authority and yet scarcely realise that there is such a thing as authority at all. And whether such a state of mind is a good one is a matter of extreme controversy, and has no place in this particular Essay. The Baroness Orczy writes her description of the somewhat " mechanical " worship very gently and with delightful sympathy.

" The gentle old priest, in simple vestments, worn threadbare with age, had entered carrying the sacred vessels, and everyone knelt for the beginning of the Mass, and the recitation of the ' Confiteor.' In respectful silence, the pious simple folk listened to the words, prescribed by the Church, not understanding their meaning, but content that they must please, since Pater Ambrosius said them."

Then there is an exquisite picture of the extraordinary thing that is the Mass, the coming of the Mighty God to be in the most intimate and fatherly way possible literally consumed by His people. It is all simple description, no hint of controversy, no hint of scepticism, a childlike faith, but not childish.

And somehow the good God must love the simple peasants ; the Sanctus Bell must be sweet music in His ears ; the Incense must arise and fill His nostrils with its precious odour.

" Then, the little bell, rung by the acolyte, announced the real bodily approach of God within the village church. Reverently all knelt down, and humble heads were bent to worship the Saviour, who at a word from Pater Ambrosius left His glorious heaven to come and sit inside that white bit of wafer, which the reverend Pater held between his fingers. A silence full of religious awe reigned, and, when the little bell had ceased to tingle, few heads dared as yet to look towards the altar, where God now truly sat enthroned."

And if it be objected that the Baroness Orczy gives too much power to the Priest, let the theological quibble dismiss itself, for it has no place in this simple and profound idea of the intimate union of God and the believer in the Mass.   And God could do much worse than choose a gentle priest to be the channel through which He would travel down to the waiting and unsophisticated peasants.

The Baroness Orczy appears to arrive at the sensible position that intricate religious mysteries have to be accepted as they stand, they must not be *thought* about too critically.

.   .   .   .

There is rather a dreadful picture of the vengeance of the Jewish moneylender.   The worm is indeed turning, and the insolent lord will have to pay dearly for the entertainment he derived by making Rosenstein swallow pig's meat.   Even the Hungarian peasant is appalled at the deadly loathing that is encased in Rosenstein's breast.

" ' Suppose, your Honour,' said the Jew, with slow emphasis, ' that I am content to pay 950,000 florins for the pleasure of seeing that man a beggar, and without a home ;   the man who amused himself, by seeing me whipped by his herdsmen, and by forcing pig's meat down my throat ?'

" Andras looked astonished, even awed, in spite of himself, by the tone of bitter, deadly hatred, which made the words come out of the Jew's mouth like the hissing of a poisonous snake."

There could scarcely be a greater contrast than these two pictures that the Baroness Orczy draws for us. The gentleness of the Mass on the one hand and the diabolical hatred of the Jew on the other. But pre-eminently is the Baroness Orczy a writer of extreme contrasts. It is that which makes her so human, so sincere, so obviously intent on truth, whether it be palatable or nauseating.

Yet the Jew in Hungary has his human qualities, he can appreciate someone who does not treat him as a dog ! It is rather an encouraging sign, for the Jewish money-lender, driven by hatred to become inhuman, can appreciate any human qualities that may be displayed towards him. We have a rather charming instance of this when Rosenstein is grateful to Andras for certain magnanimities in the past.

" ' Your Honour is the only person in the lowlands who speaks to me, as to a man, and not to a dog. You have never borrowed money of me and given me a blow as part interest. Once I fainted in the heat of the sun ; you had me taken inside your house, and tended me, till I was able to be on my feet again ; when every other peasant or lord in the country would have kicked the fainting Jew to one side."

One more quotation concerning the problem of the Jews in Eastern Europe will prove that in her " imagina-

tive " writings the Baroness Orczy is not departing from
sober fact. It is really a terrible indictment, this anni-
hilation of all the principles of human courtesy and good-
feeling. The *response* of the Jew to his odious treatment
is hardly less terrible reading. The Baroness Orczy
depicts the " cause and effect " consideration extremely
skilfully.

" The Jew in Eastern Europe stands at war with the
rest of the population ; beaten, buffeted, derided, often
injured, his only weapon is his money ; with it he gets
his revenge, on peer and peasant, and wields it merci-
lessly against all, as a poor vengeance, for all he has to
endure. He bears insults, blows, contempt of every
kind, but on the subject of money he is the master,
for he has the superior intellect, and the careful thrift,
the lack of which brings his oppressors, sooner or later,
within his clutches."

It is a little interesting to speculate how much revenge
can be engineered through money ; at any rate, the Jew
knows only too well how to play his pounds !

.   .   .   .

" A Son of the People," in my opinion, represents
satisfactorily the versatility of the Baroness Orczy. There
is that air of intimacy about her writing which I have
commented upon. There is that brilliance of description.
There is that command of writing of terror and there is
that command of writing of gentleness which is so admirably blended in her work.

If I say that the Baroness is both a romantic and a
realist, perhaps I am saying in a few words what I have
been trying to say all through this Essay. The combination of the two forms of portraiture of life seem to make
up the " entire " talented Baroness.

PART FIVE
MRS. ALFRED SIDGWICK

MRS. ALFRED SIDGWICK
Press Portrait Bureau.

PART FIVE

MRS. ALFRED SIDGWICK

MRS. ALFRED SIDGWICK manages to write an extra-ordinarily good story without taking us very far from home. We feel the story might so easily be taking place next door, that woman in the back garden ; she might quite well be someone Mrs. Sidgwick has created. That funny old man coming up from the station, his bent old shoulders, his rather pathetic mechanical bearing ; he is just like the old man we like so much in Mrs. Sidgwick's book. That rather supercilious-looking girl who would hate to be thought suburban, who would not dream of knowing any trades people, who would hardly condescend to speak to a mere clerk—Mrs. Sidgwick knows her so intimately.

In this Essay I propose to consider " The Lantern Bearers," the book in which Mrs. Sidgwick says so many things that are worth saying, and a few that are not !

.   .   .   .

It seems to me that " The Lantern Bearers " is a pleasing study of the abominably thick darkness of suburban poverty. There is no poverty that is so utterly loathsome. Suburban poverty has no affinity to the poverty of the slum. The poverty of the slum is a natural condition in quite natural surroundings. But the poverty of the

suburbs is a wholly despairing quantity, for it feels that
it has no right to exist, and, what is more hopeless, it
tries to pretend that it is not there at all. Thus, people
prefer to live in a villa because it is not quite so plebian
as life in a cottage. The villa inhabitant is a little above
the mere cottager, yet a duke can inhabit a cottage, and
yet be unable to dwell in a villa. But life in a suburban villa kills all imagination, for it is a stark deadening
reality which vibrates with the pernicious emotion of
make-believe. Mrs. Sidgwick deals with suburban poverty pretty fully, the only redeeming feature of the state
is that it implies a kind of hopeless courage, but the
courage soon develops into inevitability.

We feel that the people in the suburban villa are
really failures, even if we use the word in a rather crude
way, meaning that they have not attained to that vague
condition which is described as worldly success. The
whole atmosphere of Mrs. Sidgwick's book is a little sad,
and even depressing. I believe Mrs. Sidgwick hates
suburban people, and if she does not, she certainly ought
to. The worst of a suburb is that for some inscrutable
reason it has a pernicious effect on its inhabitants. Perhaps one reason is that suburban men are mostly automatons who merely sleep, go by the same train every
single day and come back full of hatred for the gigantic
city which callously uses them as machines. Perhaps
another reason is that suburban women are the worst
kind of arrogant snobs, self complacent, offensively res-
pectable and eminently suitable to be the wives of human
automatons. The suburbs very largely appear to collect
all the refuse that is hurled out of a great city, and the
fact that there are nice people in these horrid villa vast-
nesses merely proves that now and again human nature

defies its surroundings.   But so seldom, too greedy is the
average suburb in producing male machines and female
snobs.   The combination of the two appears to produce
children who are not as bad as might be expected.

The half-hearted apology for her grinding poverty that
Mrs. Byrne makes early on in " The Lantern Bearers "
shows that the worthy woman is merely making the best
of a very bad job.   Poor Mrs. Byrne, she is exactly like
that harassed looking woman who has just passed our
window.   But she must be respected because she does
not want her daughter to be too angry and despairing
about the poverty that overshadows everything.

Mrs. Sidgwick seems to me to contrast the point of
view of the daughter and the guardedness of the mother
very skilfully.

" I believe you like being poor, Mummy,' Helga said
one morning.

" The two ladies were in the little back kitchen, and
they were washing their own clothes.   Mrs. Byrne
stood at the wringing machine and put piece after piece
through it.   She looked hot, poor woman, but not
cross.

" ' Poverty has a good as well as a bad side,' she
said.   ' You must know how to meet it.' "

But poor Helga knows too much about the bad side of
it, why the horrid condition means that you cannot
have pretty frocks or go to dances—all so terrible for a
young girl.

" ' I know all about the bad side,' said Helga, in her
ignorance.   ' We can't have anything we want, and

Dad is always fretting, and you work like a galley slave, and I—if I go to this dance I can't dance. I've never had any lessons.' "

Poverty is hateful for the young. When we are older we don't mind so much or we have got so used to it, that it has become part of ourselves and—the world that is looming nearer and nearer denotes that poverty is riches ; and when we are old the paradox does not seem so absurd, so illusory, so of the nature of a vague and unsatisfying promise. So well does Mrs. Sidgwick bring out the resigned attitude of Mrs. Byrne in contrast to the impatience of the young girl.

The rather sordid villa life is the result of a " deal " that may be a mixture of folly and sharp practice or merely treachery. It is never easy to say whether Mrs. Sidgwick means that Mr. Ashley is a scoundrel or whether he merely took advantage of the lesser ability of Mr. Byrne. But the event that led to the suburban poverty is this :

" ' Mr. Ashley dissolved the partnership when every penny your father possessed was sunk in Eonion, the Everlasting Wood.' "

Then we get the few lines of dialogue which leave us wondering whether Mr. Ashley was after all merely discrete. At the end of the lines of dialogue there is that rather nasty truism that " friends " so often drop out when prosperity is transformed into failure. The lines are so human, so true to life, that I quote them in full.

" ' At that time Eonion had not begun to pay.'

" ' Does it pay now ?'

" ' Enormously. Mr. Ashley is making a fortune out of it.'

" ' But if Dad had money in it—'

" ' I know ; but I can't explain all the ins and outs.'

" ' Poor Dad ! But why didn't his friends help him ?'

" ' Some of them did. They found him his present berth.'

" ' But where are they all ? Why do we never see any one ?'

" ' When you are as poor as we are you drop out,' said Mrs. Byrne, and turned to her basket of clothes again."

There is nothing like failure to sift the true friends from the false, it is perhaps a subtle blessing that carries with it some small compensation.

Mrs. Sidgwick gives a vivid picture of the isolation of the suburbs. The suburbs are very melancholy places unless you happen to be right in the pseudo society that exists in cheap and undistinguished little cliques that abound with the various organisations. There is the dancing clique, which usually consists of a few short-haired women, a few long-haired men and a sprinkling of fat and vulgar mothers. There is the religious clique which endeavours to worship God in a red brick church which is so hideous often that art and worship seem to be in violent opposition. There is the lonely clique, the outsiders of whom no notice is taken, the mere nobodies, those who are as utterly unknown to the rest of the world as cannibals on an obscure island in the Pacific. To this latter clique belonged the Byrnes. Mrs. Sidgwick shows us the rather miserable business.

" The little house in which the Byrnes lived was tucked away at the extreme edge of the suburb, where houses ended and fields began.   The family was not an object of interest or curiosity as it would have been in a country neighbourhood."

There are too many people in the suburbs for uninteresting and curious people to be taken notice of, the better class people are too occupied with their own affairs to have time to worry about their poorer neighbours.   Far from showing any kind of kindness to the Byrnes, the well-to-do neighbours merely felt irritated that Mrs. Byrne should not only be so poor, but look so unsuccessful.

" On one side of the house was an avenue of trees and a dairy farm ; on the other side two or three small houses usually to let.   Beyond that came detached houses of a better class, inhabited by people who never learned the name of the woman who hung out her own washing, but regarded her as a blot on their decorous neighbourhood and wished that fate would remove her."

I do not think that Mrs. Sidgwick is the least unfair in her attitude to suburban people.   In fact, she really lets them down far more lightly than they deserve.   But their self complacency will hardly allow them to realise this undeserved clemency !

Having said something about the suburbs and suburban people, it will be merely logical to follow Mrs. Sidgwick from the general down to the particular.   Mr. Byrne is a most depressing creature.   Life, that unscrupulous fighter, has beaten him.   Life is chuckling just round the corner ; each day he makes Mr. Byrne a little more depressed.   If it was not for Mrs. Byrne, life would have laughed uproariously, for he would have gained a signal victory. I rather think that Life thoroughly enjoys the stream of hopeless men who shuffle home every night from the City. I rather think that Life is a firm friend of Death, but I think that Death is more good natured, when he sees that the bent back, the haggard face, cannot stand any more, he gently intervenes and Life has to give up his victim.

Mrs. Sidgwick writes sympathetically of Mr. Byrne. In so many houses there are the Mr. Byrne's.

" Helga could not remember much about the time when her father was flourishing. His misfortune had unstrung him, and his child's unhappy experience was that all the fun ended when he came back from the City. He was not unkind or bad tempered, but his outlook was so gloomy that if you were mercurial yourself it depressed you. His wife's strong, placid nature resisted his influence, but, though she loved him, even she dreaded his foreboding view of life. He seemed unable to look forward to anything but future miseries."

When a man has lost the power of thinking there may be a better future, even if the present is inky black, there seems to be no hope for him. It is deadly despair, that fearful emotion which makes the Agony in Gethsemane seem marvellous optimism. It would be perhaps interesting to speculate on what would have happened had Christ in The Garden given way to despair. Mrs. Sidgwick by her dialogue seems to imply that Mr. Byrne has his Gethsemane, but there is no Light playing around it, for cold despair has quenched that Light.

" ' Are you tired, Dad ?' Helga said to-night, as she went towards him, for she saw that he was leaning back in his chair with half-closed eyes.

" ' Not worse than usual,' he said, ' at my age . . '

" ' You're not old, Dad.'

" ' I'm fifty. That's old for a man who has failed. They'll soon say I'm past work and then—Heaven help us.' "

The practical optimism of Mrs. Byrne in contrast to this despairing attitude of her husband is delightfully depicted by the retort that Mrs. Byrne makes.

" ' Certainly Heaven will help us if we help ourselves,' said Mrs. Byrne calmly."

Very soon Mrs. Sidgwick conducts us right into the centre of the family life of the Byrnes. It is a charming picture, and so homely that we wonder if Mrs. Sidgwick has not been in our own house while we have been out. A nice little mixture of threatening bills and dinner on the table.

" She went to the mantelpiece, removed a little dust of tobacco her husband had left there, looked through some letters stacked at one corner, and found a printed blue one that she handed to her husband.

" ' The third demand,' she said. ' If it is not paid before Tuesday—'

" Mr. Byrne groaned and put the horrid thing into his pocket. Helga opened the door and put her head into the room.

" ' Dinner is quite ready,' she said. ' Have you told Dad about the wedding gown ?'

" ' Not yet,' said Mrs. Byrne."

.   .   .   .

Foreigners quite frequently complain that the English are cold. They would be more accurate if they said we were shy. What the foreigner does not seem to understand is that the Englishman nearly always waits for the other person. Once the other person has made the initial move, all is well, and foreigners then marvel at our complete and unrestrained good humour. The English are a nation of " waiters," which is due to conceit and shyness—not an unusual combination. Modesty the Englishman has no conception of ; he is so certain of his own superiority that he strikes all foreigners as being incapable of avoiding an unpleasant attitude of well bred sniffing. Now Helga Byrne gets a good taste of English coldness when she goes to a dance at Wimbledon. Being shy, the girl is naturally left alone ; the dance being at an English house, it is merely logical that strangers will be entirely left alone. The English have a genius of clannishness, and the fact that England is an island has no little to do with it. Mrs. Sidgwick gives an example of this English chilliness in an arresting description of Helga sitting alone while the gay dancers float by. So like Life, with passers floating by and others watching the floating.

" The musicians struck up a waltz, an enchanting waltz that set Helga longing to move to it, and everyone except Helga and the matrons began to dance again. The girl tried valiantly not to mind, or, rather, not to show that she minded."

And the worst loneliness is that kind when we are watched, when we feel the gay throng rather angry that there is someone who is not quite enjoying the pageant. Possibly the Crucifixion would not have been so remorseless if there had not been the crowds to watch the spectacle of the Lonely God being " killed " by His own creations.

The world is always a little angry that God didn't get off the Cross, because it has meant that the world was so thoroughly beaten.

" If only she could have hidden behind other people she would have felt quite calm and comfortable. It was the publicity of her loneliness that made it so hard to bear."

How we hate being conspicuous when we are left out ; how we love being conspicuous when we are watched by an admiring throng that cheers and cheers until we tell them the naked truth and the cheering is turned to jeering. The real and essential reason of Helga's loneliness was, of course, the fact that she was at a dance where there was a very bad hostess.

" Mrs. Warwick had neither husband nor children to help her take care of her guests, and the two nieces on whom she depended were entirely occupied in taking care of themselves and their intimate friends."

Poor hostesses in England are rather unusual, and Helga seems to have been unusually unlucky.

I have already said that Mrs. Sidgwick has a good deal to say about suburbs, and that they come in for some harsh but not unfair treatment. Probably the deadening life in a suburb is a good deal responsible for the appalling lack of imagination that so many suburban people manifest. And nothing is more conducive to snobbery than lack of imagination. The snob is so engrossed with his own excellence and merit that the super excellence of his neighbour merely appears to him something quite beneath his notice. Mrs. Sidgwick put a typical snobbish speech into the mouth of a typical suburban girl. The girl is not exactly to be blamed for her snobbishness, for it has quite evidently been handed down to her almost as a tradition. And there is probably no tradition that is so hard to eradicate, for it is a tradition that is founded on long and accumulated years of a false imagination, or, much more likely, no imagination at all. The words are put into the mouth of a girl named Marcella and she quite evidently has no qualms of conscience at using them.

> " ' I know who these Byrnes are. We live quite near them, but we should not seek their acquaintance. The man is a clerk and the woman hangs out her own washing.' "

Quite enough to damn them in the eyes of aristocratic suburbia.

Though Mrs. Byrne cannot be blamed for hanging out her own washing, she might be severely brought to task for her nonsense in objecting to her daughter talking to a young man. But Mrs. Byrne is merely a rather foolish mother, who, having experienced all her own emotions, does not realise that her daughter has the same emotions.

> " Mrs. Byrne looked unhappy.
> " ' I have always taught you most carefully how a girl should conduct herself,' she said. ' Surely you know that to sit in a garden with one young man—' "

But the " dreadful " story goes further. Helga, with more than a touch of modernism, actually drove back in a carriage alone with the selfsame young man !

Mrs. Sidgwick is very clever at depicting contrasts.

The difference in outlook between Mrs. Byrne and her daughter. The melancholy of Mr. Byrne, the practical efficiency of Mr. Byrne. It is all so admirably conceived, we see all the time the individualities of the Byrne family ; we realise that a small villa may hold so many emotions that man could not count them ; we are reconciled to the fact that in one family differences of opinion are inevitable, that the blood relationship does not in any way indicate singleness of outlook.

There is a certain amount of hopeless courage about the Byrne family ; in spite of the isolation of their life they are not beaten. Even when old Mr. Byrne goes to bed dead tired, we are perfectly certain that the next day will find him trudging to the City. Mrs. Byrne does not in the least mind really what her neighbours think of her, a reason why they are annoyed at her presence. Silent contempt on the part of alleged inferiors is, of course, most annoying. Sometimes Mrs. Sidgwick gives us a most pleasing glimpse of home life ; something that vaguely suggests drawn blinds and hot toast, the kettle boiling over—outside the dear old street lamps beginning to be lighted, that they may pilot wayfarers through the night. Street lamps, we love them, they guard us until the morning, kind of guardian angels, they look in the distance like stars which have fallen to the earth.

It seems as if nearly every novelist who has ever existed has some distinct conception of love. In this book I have endeavoured to show how the emotion is considered by such diverse novelists as Miss Sheila Kaye-Smith and Miss Ethel M. Dell. Mrs. Sidgwick tells us how Helga regards love. It is almost as a kind of beautiful thinking, a sort of echo, a looking backward to concrete acts, and then in imagination going over them again and again.

The kind of emotion that makes the lover say to himself—
How soft her eyes looked ; the kind of emotion that makes
the lover say to herself—His mouth is so adorable when
he is about to kiss me.

> " ' You know how it is,' she said. ' You lie awake
> and you think of every word and every look, and you
> remember all the little things—the way you fill your
> pipe, and the feel of your coat—the silliest things—
> and you wish and wish, till one thinks your spirit must
> come because it is called and wanted so."

It is a kind of lovely memory, something that will
satisfy just a little should the reality never happen again,
almost as we remember the sweet summer sky when we
are enveloped in such a thick fog that we are quite sure
the sky has gone away vexed with humanity.

Now for a contrast. The love of an elderly woman for
her husband of many years. Again a looking backward,
but a contented knowledge that there is a very distinct
present as well. Mrs. Byrne consoles her husband ; her
love has in it an instinct of maternity. Rather different
from the love of Helga, which has in it the instinct of
passion which has yet to be satisfied.

> " She sat down beside him now and put her hand on
> his with a caressing touch. The love this elderly woman
> felt for this broken man was so real and pititful that she
> ached with it. When she was a girl it had sometimes
> made her sad to read that love dies with youth because
> youth goes and many things go with it."

But for Mrs. Byrne love is the real thing for satisfaction
has not killed it. It has borne the reaction of sex, it has

been of sex but transcending sex. Probably love is sex plus transcended sex eliminating the deadening reaction which proves pseudo love.

" But now she was old, and knew that the one divine light of life still burnt clearly. The flame was of a different colour, doubtless from that consuming her child's heart, since memory, time and pity all helped to feed it. But it illumined a fate that without it would have been like ashes."

When Mr. Byrne loses his work we are shown that of all the terrible positions in which a poor man may find himself, that of being middle-aged and out of work, is not the least poignant. The hopeless tramp from office to office, the interviews that always end in the same way, the weary return to the nearly desperate family, the tricks of fate that take a delight in trying to make things worse by introducing fresh trials and shocks. All the tale of misfortune Mrs. Sidgwick depicts carefully. The old man, no more the slender comfort of a routine job, no more the certainty of a moderate dinner in the evening and a night's rest to oil the machine for the duties of the next day.

" He was an elderly gentleman fallen on evil days. The manual labour always wanted he could not do. The clerk's work he understood he could not get. Every night he came back with the same story. The desks were all full, the doors were all closed. Trade was bad and firms were dismissing men, not taking them on."

A very weary round when Life seems to be but an unending misery. Mrs. Sidgwick makes us very sorry for poor Mr. Byrne, and he stands out so prominently that the sorrow almost hurts.

I hope that I have made it plain that in " The Lantern Bearers " Mrs. Sidgwick has written a domestic story. Her situations are rather ordinary ; they are not for the most part highly dramatic. A parallelism of courage and failure pervades the whole atmosphere. Mrs. Sidgwick is never really profound, she evidently relies on commonsense. She can handle love very reasonably without philosophising very much about it. " The Lantern Bearers " are live people, and as I have already said, could be seen in the garden at the back.

Mrs. Sidgwick writes of middle class people, their life rather like their surroundings are also middle class. That is the people who are of no apparent importance in the world except the " world " that is a suburban villa.

But the essence of Mrs. Sidgwick's skill is that the unimportant Byrne's have a history that touches on the emotions. Out of rather slender material Mrs. Sidgwick weaves a delicate garment. And we have no objection to being enveloped in it !

PART SIX
MISS CYNTHIA STOCKLEY

MISS CYNTHIA STOCKLEY
Elliott & Fry, Ltd.

PART SIX

MISS CYNTHIA STOCKLEY

THERE are certain novels for which we ought to take a ticket! For they convey us on delightful journeys, far beyond the confines of our previous journeys. I do not believe that we are half grateful enough to the novelists who give us so much more than mere glimpses of foreign countries. We pay no more tribute to the novelist who takes us no further than Balham, than to the writer of fiction who leaves us gasping in the appalling heat of an African sun. And this is surely a little ungrateful, a little unenterprising. For the travel novelist is a very true friend ; he knows that we cannot afford to see much of the world ; he knows that much of our life is passed gazing on the changing colours of the basement steps, he knows that if we could, we would sail to the sun, that we might look down on the glorious mass spread far beneath which is the earth. And, being a kindly soul, he takes us on a journey in a book and adds, as though we were not already indebted enough to him, a story so that our pleasure is doubled.

Miss Cynthia Stockley is a travel novelist—right away we go with her to that terrible and mysterious continent which is Africa. I propose to examine something of her art in " The Claw." Whatever I may say hereafter, I feel grateful to her in the way that I say *all* readers should be grateful to travel novelists.

．　．　．　．　．　．　．　．　．

The whole atmosphere that vibrates round Miss Stockley is something that can be described as violent. There is violent discomfort, violent love, violent hatred, violent scandal. At the very beginning of the book there is violent discomfort, the physical misery that permeates an English girl riding across the African veld in a post-cart. Africa delights in being violent, it takes a savage delight in shaking a post-cart so that the occupant may know the acme of agony that can be contained in rough journeying.

" There was no rest or comfort anywhere in that post-cart. In spite of my chiffon veil, I could feel the fine road dust powdering thickly on to my charming face. Mosquitoes sped down silently from strong-holds in the hooped tent of the cart, and without even a warning serenade took long draughts of my nice young blood through the linen sleeves of my blouse. A hundred grass ticks, having at various times of outspan made convenient entry through open work brown silk stockings, chewed at my ankles, causing exquisite irritation not to be assuaged by a violent application of finger-nails."

This delightful description proves an unalterable law, that woman will wear silk stockings under any conditions, no matter whether she be on the veld or in the howling wilderness of some smart hotel. Traveller or vampire or both, woman must clad her legs in silk ! But even if silk stockings are the way to infinite irritation the wonder of Africa compensates the owner of them.

" At six o'clock the heat was still intense, and the western sky resembled a vast frameless picture, daubed in primitive colours, slashed and gashed with reds and yellows. An hour later the sun shot past the horizon like a red-hot cannon ball aimed at the other side of the world, and for a short time the land was suffused in wilder lights of orange, and the skies seemed streaked with blood."

For Miss Saurin, the charming English girl that Miss Stockley has created, does not mind so long as she is in Africa, under the gorgeous skies, with the limitless veld stretching away and away, an ocean of land falling over a precipice and meeting the sky just where the eye could reach its furthest limit.

" It seemed to me then to be possible to disregard the discomforts of the day, and to forget what terrors the night might hold, by just succumbing to the charm and the magic of this wonderful great empty land. I was content to be in Africa."

It is not very often that we are privileged to read of the emotions of a girl left alone in the middle of an African night. Miss Stockley writes of the experience with great vividness. It is a clever description of that kind of phantastic background that we " see " when it is dark, the strange and unaccountable shadows, the spectre land that would look so ordinary by day.

" Began then for me the strangest night of all my

life. In the midst of the thick darkness there suddenly
and unwarrantably appeared between the branches of
trees, taller than any I had seen on the whole journey,
a wraith-like new moon white as a milk opal. It peered
through the black trees like a ghost that has lost its
soul and seeks for it in desolate places. It shed no light
at all, but just hovered there, peering, paling the light
of the stars and etching into view things that had better
have been left hidden."

In such a situation it is difficult for the soul to realise
that it is still chained to the body, that it has not left the
earth, that it has not left far behind the poor dead body ;
it is almost impossible to conceive that the same earth
which holds an African night also holds a sordid street in
Wapping ! But possibly it is even more difficult for the
street in Wapping to imagine the desperate magic of an
African night.

.   .   .   .

Miss Stockley deals quite uncompromisingly with all
kinds of situations. I do not think that it is unfair to say
that too many white men think that it is an excellent
virtue to thrash and kick black men. It is the primitive
instinct of the white man, his feeling of contempt for the
black, his proposition that only may the black man inhabit so much of the earth as the white man considers to
be good for him.

Miss Saurin has of course been badly looked after by her
black driver, but, this is where my contention comes in,
her rescuer's first instinct is to thrash and kick the black
driver. Very probably the black driver deserved it, but
one of the most hateful attributes of the white man is his
predisposition to chastising those who are coloured. He

considers that the black man should be thrashed because
he is black, he has no right to object to being kicked,
because a white man has a primitive right to kick black
flesh. But if a black man attempts to attack a white
man, let him be lynched, let him be taught that the
sacred white man, the sacred Englishman, is so holy, so
pure, that on no account must the black show any resentment.

Miss Stockley brings it out well, how the big white man
is so delightfully chivalrous for a poor unprotected white
woman, that he must quickly thrash the black man.

" ' There, there—don't cry, for Heaven's sake don't
cry—it's all right now—you're quite safe—I'll take care
of you. And I'll hammer that brute within an inch of
his life to-morrow morning,' he added savagely."

It is a little disturbing to discover that this chivalrous
protector of helpless women is a thorough cad. It makes
the blacks question a *little* whether it is a mark of merit
to have been kicked by a white, whether, after all, whites
are so superior that they must travel in separate tram-cars,
ride in separate compartments and be prevented from
walking down certain streets, lest they contaminate the
" white " scandal-loving women and the " white " gos-
siping husbands.

Miss Stockley has a habit of making quite a profound
remark when the opportunity presents itself. Here is one.
" Nothing is strange on the veld." In my opinion
this comment suggests an inexorable law. Nothing is
really strange when one is at grips with nature. Nature
freed from the abominable artificialities of civilisation, is
quite open with itself, unashamed, and definitely con-

temptuous of man-made conventions. The actual incident that leads up to the remark is the somewhat unusual spectacle of a man and a woman sitting under the stars when the woman does not even know the name of her companion.

" It did not seem in the least strange to be sitting there under the stars in that wild place, taking possession of a large meal with a man who did not know my name nor I his."

It did not seem strange because the situation is freed from society conventions, freed from the harsh gossips of unclean lepers, freed from the hypocrisy which masquerades as morality, but above all " nothing is strange on the veld."

But as soon as Miss Saurin is among civilised beings again she is in the centre of gossip and scandal. It seems to prove my contention that humanity is only vile when it is mixed up with humanity. It is a little humiliating, a little depressing, but not hopeless. For humanity with humanity is not its true self, it poses, it likes to be thought naughty, it loves to be daring, but all the time it really wonders—is it well with the soul—is it well ? People like to be thought bad because it seems to prove that they have not lost all their attractions ! At the same time they like to find fault with other people, for it is a subtle delight to feel that others are so much weaker and foolish than we are. It is a curious piece of psychology this wishing to be thought bad or rather somewhat indiscreet, while roundly condemning the same wishes in the person just across the table. What I mean, in a word, is that mankind is not naturally bad, it is artificially so, especially that kind of society which is gathered together in small localities—the Hill stations in Mr. Kipling's books, the society in Miss Stockley's book which is being discussed in this Essay.

I hope that a few quotations will show how cleverly Miss Stockley deals with the detestable scandal-loving people amongst whom Miss Saurin finds herself. They are a miserable lot of people, apparently quite unscrupulous and yet perhaps the isolation of Africa, the lack of outside subjects in a small community has quite a lot to do with the hateful state of affairs.

Miss Saurin has the good sense to dislike the " horrid " people. They are discussing a soldier who is not quite a soldier—a good fellow—but—well—not quite *pukka*.

" It appeared that Anthony Kinsella was not an army man as English people understand the term.

" ' *Almost*, but *not* quite,' said Gerald Deshon, ' he is one of us.' "

Miss Saurin then asks an indiscreet question, forgetting that jealous and frumpy females are waiting like vultures ready to pounce at the least opportunity to suggest indelicate lines of thought.

" ' But why does he wear turquoise earrings ?' I asked involuntarily, thinking no one but Lord Gerry was listening.

" I was mistaken.

" ' Some woman stuck them in his ears, I suppose,' said Mrs. Valetta fiercely ; and she and Miss Cleeve glared at me across their cards."

Miss Saurin, not quite used to the atmosphere of the

English in our colonies, grows sick of them.   She frankly
says so, and brings forth a retort which proves, as I have
already suggested, that humanity is sound when it really
needs to be.

" Do the Fort George men spend their evenings
talking scandal also ?"

There was absolute silence, and then all the men began
to grin."

Then comes the true and thoughtful answer by Maurice
Stair, the man who afterwards marries Miss Saurin.

" It takes all sorts of men to make a war.   Perhaps
if we are no good *now* we may be when the fighting comes
along."

The reply is an echo of the immortal verse of Mr.
Kipling.

" Then it's Tommy this, an' Tommy that, an' Tommy
        ow's yer soul ?
    But it's thin red line of 'eroes when the drums
        begin to roll,
    The drums begin to roll, my boys, the drums begin
        to roll,
    Oh, it's thin red line of 'eroes when the drums begin
        to roll."

On the next day Miss Saurin experiences some more
gossip—gossip which has become the utterances of feminine devils, whose proper environment would be a per-
manent billet in the dustbin.   It would be an excellent
thing if gossip could be made a criminal offence, even if it
is in no way of the nature of libel.

The few lines that I quote makes it quite evident that Miss Stockley has made a keen observation of the methods that women employ when they are engaged in the truly feminine pastime of blackguarding other women. It is quite probable that had not Christ been crucified on a cross by men, He would have been crucified on a cross of gossip erected by women. And the latter would probably have been more painful.

" Consumed with curiosity I addressed a query to Judy, sitting next to me.

" ' That person ?' said she, looking another way. ' She calls herself Rookwood, I believe.'

" ' What has she done ?' I asked. It was so very evident that the poor wretch had done something.

" ' Oh, don't ask me,' said Judy in a far-away voice.

" But Mrs. Skeffington-Smythe, who sat on the other side, was not so reserved.

" ' Do you see that big fair man with her ? That is Captain Rookwood. Handsome, isn't he ? She lives with him.'

" ' Do you mean she is married to him ?'

" ' Married to him—not at all. She is married to a man called Geach, in Cape Town, but she ran away from him with George Rookwood, and they have been living together for six months now. Her husband by way of revenge refuses to divorce her. Isn't it insolent of her to come here amongst us ?' "

Which, of course, infers the pretty little problem, whether free love is more despicable than unrestrained scandal mongering.

. . . .

If it is true to say that Miss Stockley has a habit of making profound observations, it is also equally true to say that she has a habit of writing smart retorts. Especially is this apparent when she is in the midst of the gossip-loving community about which I have just written. Miss Saurin determines to shock the self-complacent community just a little.

> " ' I got more compliments for my coffee. Everyone said it was delicious. Greedy people asked for second or even third cups. Colonel Blow was heard to state that he had never tasted anything like it since he was in Paris a hundred years ago.' "

Miss Saurin then drops her bombshell, a nasty explosion, causing at least ten minutes dismay.

> " ' That is just where I learned to make it,' I said gaily. ' In my rackety days in the *Quartier*.'
> " Everyone looked amazed, and I suppose it was rather an amazing thing to say.
> " ' In your what days ?' asked Miss Cleeve faintly.
> " And Mrs. Valetta said in a curious voice : ' Can you possibly mean the Latin Quarter of Paris ?'
> " ' I can indeed,' quoth I affably. ' I once had a studio there for six months, and all the art students used to come in the evenings and make coffee and welsh rarebit, and every delicious imaginable thing."

Miss Saurin is well able to turn the tables on the " horrid people " among whom she finds herself. The dialogue that Miss Stockley creates appears to exactly harmonise with the type of person she is writing of. It is a characteristic of her art, a harmonious blending of character and the effect of certain situations on that character. Miss Saurin can be brilliant because she dislikes the people among whom she moves ; among people she likes she would probably be quite commonplace.

From this clever and yet superficial conversation Miss Stockley can amazingly quickly switch over to the violent passion of love. Love which turns Africa into a paradise of ecstatic dreams ; love which soothes with a soft and indescribable sweetness ; love which has the self-same thrill, whether it be in the midst of a vast continent, in the shaded lights of a huge ball room, or in the middle of the solemn ocean through which the giant ship so persistently ploughs.

" Ah ! It is a most wonderful and exquisite thing to be alone in the empty, silent, moonlit world with the man you love, and who loves you.

" ' Come, love,' said Anthony to me, simply and softly, and drew me down the stairway. In the kindly darkness he kissed me again in a strong, sweet, wonderful way, and for one more radiant moment I felt the almost anguished joy—half terror and half exquisite peace—that comes to a girl who, loving for the first time, finds herself in the arms of the one right man in all the world for her.

" ' Say you love me,' he passionately whispered, and I as passionately whispered back ' I love you—I love you. There is no one in the world like you.' "

It is a dream that is never repeated. The first of any experience is always the most memorable—the first book that an author publishes, the first picture that an artist paints ; the first prize that a school-boy gets ; the first moment when a woman knows that she is loved ; the first time that a man knows he loves. It may be that subsequent events are more outstanding, that a second book or picture entirely eclipses the first ; but there is not the same thrill, the same sense of a desperate adventure, the same breaking in on a new world—the same incredible feeling of wonder, the same indescribable sense of achievement.

So well, so sympathetically does Miss Stockley deal with this splendid " first " emotion. Miss Saurin is a " good Catholic." Her first act, when alone, is to pay tribute to God.

> " Alone in my room at last, I threw myself down on my knees and thanked God in broken words for my happiness."

It is ever the same—great happiness or great agony—up in Heaven God receives a Eucharist or a prayer.

Miss Saurin's emotions are beautifully written—their religious significance, the wish to shout the good news aloud from the house-tops, the glorious climax to an adventure the end of which seemed as problematical.

> " With the rosary between my fingers and the lovely Latin words of the Angelical Salutation on my lips, I thought of my mother, too, and longed passionately for her to know of the wonderful thing that had come to me, so that even in my prayers my thoughts flew out from me across the rolling spaces of stars to the still place of peace where my faith told me her soul rested, waiting ; and when at last I rose from my knees it was with a strange feeling that she knew."

Again, it is necessary to write of Miss Stockley in another

mood. Dark tragic misery, when Miss Saurin has married
the man who was not her first found lover.

. . . .

If Miss Stockley can describe the violence of love, the
violence of despair finds her equally an excellent " pain-
ter." The exquisite torture that is inflicted on Miss
Saurin by the supposed death of her lover is so minutely
chronicled that the reading is almost physically painful.
Africa is turned from a land of exquisite delight to a land
of abnormal misery. Africa has done her worst, but she
has been unable to claim a decisive victory.

> " For three months I lay at the door of death,
> craving entry into the place that held all I loved. But
> Africa had not done with me. She dragged me back
> from the dark, healed my sick body with her sunshine
> and cooled my fevers with her sparkling air."

It seems to Miss Saurin almost as if Africa had wished
to be revenged on her, revenged on humanity that dared
to come and disturb its vast quietnesses. A kind of
mysterious revenge of a wild country against the inroads
of civilisation with its accompanyings of malice and guile.

> " ' In strange moments a kind of exquisitely bitter
> contentment possessed me at having paid with the last
> drop of my heart's blood the price she exacts from the
> children of civilisation who come walking with careless
> feet in her wild secret places."

I have mentioned before that Miss Stockley can write
something that can be described as beautiful. Particularly is this so when she writes of people who pass across
our life and are gone. They come right into our life, we

are gripped by their harmonious outlook with our own and then one day they are gone. That little speck in the distance, almost out of sight, we shall never see that person again, the little speck has died away, we are horribly alone. Another speck in the far, far distance it comes nearer and nearer, it soon proves to be a new friend, but do not think, new friend, that we are ungrateful or proud, but that tiny vanished speck has taken so much of us away.

" That is the way in Africa. People come into your life, live in almost family intimacy with you, learn (very often) the very inmost secrets of your heart, share joys and sorrows with you, then pass on and are lost to you for ever. Only here and there you grasp a hand that you can hold over hills and seas though darkness hide you one from another and leagues divide until the end."

There is a charming mysticism in such a thought, and it is perhaps not an exaggeration to think that such a " binding " can exist when one has passed on, so that he is nowhere that can be held by mortal sight. At least the thought is not unprofitable. So many of us would end it all suddenly, if we thought that a reunion beyond the grave was impossible.

Yet again Miss Stockley writes a really lovely description of the magnetism of the veld, its strange reaction to human emotions, its melancholy and its soothing propensities, its exhilaration and its peculiar message of stability and peace. Miss Stockley's picture is simple, but it is a simplicity which has in it that which is delicate.

" A strange thing about the veld is that if you stare

long at it when you are happy your eyes will fill with tears, and an indefinable sorrow surges in your veins. But go to it when you are wretched, and its beauty will lay shadowy hands on you and bless you and enfold you, and something will wing its way into your heart like a white heron of peace, and nestling there give you comfort and courage."

When Miss Saurin has married Maurice Stair we get a very grim piece of realism. For Stair is a cad and a liar, and Miss Saurin determines that the marriage shall admit of no normal intimacy. The marriage has been entered into by means of a vile trick, for Maurice Stair has pretended that Anthony Kinsells is dead when there is certainty of the fact. There is no hiding of the horrible conditions of such a marriage.

" ' I was fighting with Maurice Stair for my soul. I could not love him ; he was an unworthy traitor and liar, but I was his wife and I wanted his home and name to shelter me from sin. Only I would take them on no other conditions than those I had named to him.' "

There is a long grim struggle, desire and its fight against tenacity, an awful disharmony in a condition the very essence of which is harmony.

" Long, long we stayed there, fighting that fight. I cannot remember all that was said. I only knew that once I sank into a chair almost fainting, that once there was a time when he wept like a child, his head on the table. At another he reviled me until my knees shook and cursed the hour I had set foot in his life."

But this is merely a prelude to the violent storm. Miss Stockley takes us along the road of grim realism by easy stages.

> " There was another night when, after bitter taunts had been hurled like poisoned arrows round the room, he tore the bed clothes and pillows from my bed, and the gowns and hangings from the walls and flung them in heaps and tatters into the rain sodden yard."

It is a marriage that at least has the virtue of excitement ! Perhaps they are needed, as Miss Stockley tells us " after such incidents came intervals of days and weeks in which we never opened lips to each other."

We reach something that can be called the climax of hatred when Miss Saurin storms out three terrible words at her husband. At the dreadful moment when she learns that the frightful injury to her little kitten has been caused by her husband's diabolical temper.

> " The man took the kitten from me and went from the room, and I followed ; but as I passed Maurice Stair I whispered three words at him, with terrible eyes.

> " ' *Take it then* !' "

The " It " is poison—poison that twists and contorts, poison that would send an agonising death.

. . . .

I hope that it may be evident from the examination that I have made of something of Miss Stockley's approach to the Art of Fiction, that the word violent was not a misapplication.

Miss Stockley writes of beautiful things " beautifully." She writes of cruel things " cruelly." She writes of real things—all the time. " The Claw " is a tragedy because it deals with that most tragic of all tragedies—a tragic marriage. Miss Stockley does not allow her imagination to saunter too far. Quite a number of novelists allow such rein to the imagination that the quality leads to invention. With a novelist of the realist type such a journey is fraught with grave consequences.

But Miss Stockley keeps control of her story, for she knows that though limits of realism are not limitless, yet nevertheless they are not easily limited. Miss Stockley keeps a middle course, but the middle course does not become merely lukewarmness.

Again I believe that Miss Stockley is best described as a " violent writer," but the violence is always a sane violence. Perhaps the best form of drama.

MRS. HENRY DE LA PASTURE

PART SEVEN

MRS. HENRY DE LA PASTURE

MRS. DE LA PASTURE takes us back to days tha tare gone for ever. For the days that existed before the war are as much gone as the days that existed when Nero was foolish enough to think he could destroy Christianity by burning Christians, thereby proving a " law " that one burnt Christian is more useful to Christianity than a thousand Christians who are not burnt.

When I say that Mrs. De La Pasture writes of a period that is irrevocably gone, I speak of something that many well-meaning people entirely miss. They deplore the damage caused by the war, they deplore the countless men who were violently killed, as if time in the least matters to a soul, they deplore the fact that bacon will never be so cheap again, but they miss the fundamental fact that civilisation has quite changed since the war. Or, if we narrow down the statement to fit Mrs. De La Pasture's actual locality, it has completely changed London. I shall attempt to show this by saying something of her book, " The Man from America," quite a good deal of which has to do with London before the war.

Of course, in the modern sense of the word Mrs. De La ·e is old-fashioned, and modern people are rather icially inclined to distrust anything that is old-fashioned. It is a subtle form of optimism which quite unconsciously permeates the everlasting present. If a young man or a young woman did not think that his own generation knew very much better than the preceding one, we should probably find youth creating a dangerous attitude to life, which might be philosophically defined as pessimism. But this is no reason for denying a sentimental regret at the passing of old-fashioned customs to be quite rational. It is not mere sentimental gush which deplores the passing of the London hansom cab ; it is indeed a melancholy fact that in all walks of life machinery is pushing out animal locomotion. There was something picturesque about a horse omnibus ; a motor omnibus is a useful and hideous monstrosity. The London of Mrs. De La Pasture was a less barbarous place than the London of to-day, but the humanity of London seems to have been much the same as the humanity of the days of Nero— some good, a great deal bad, quite a lot neither good nor bad, merely abominably mediocre.

Mrs. De La Pasture has a delicate method of writing, almost as if she felt a kind of reverence for the pen which conveys her thoughts to paper. She is, if one can use the term, *well-bred* in literature ; she does not take liberties with the divine art ; she approaches with humility, so much so that sometimes her situations seem to fall short of their logical climax. I shall endeavour to show something of her art by means of a discussion of " The Man from America," a really delicious piece of work—almost as delicious as a delicate picture.

. . . .

There seems to be a distinct tendency in much m
fiction to gib at any kind of straightforward descri
The art of description by suggestion, clever as it i

often, seems to have been carried to such an exaggerated degree that the novelist is positively *afraid* of description by description. I refer very largely to description of people, the direct method being seldom employed. Description of places by description still of course exists, but it has largely lost the quality of *simplicity* that Mrs. De La Pasture invests it with.

Mrs. De La Pasture gives rather a charming descripton of the Vicomte's home in Devon. Simplicity in this case does all that is necessary. For English scenery is best described without attempts at brilliance ; it is a kind of scenery which ill harmonises with lurid pen pictures, however well they may be done.

" Honeycott Manor lay on the sunny side of the Cullaway hills, near the village of Luscombe, and midway between the small but ancient towns of Remberton in Somerset and Domaford in Devon."

So much for the topographical setting of this delightful house. The more intimate picture is done with care and simplicity.

" Doors and windows alike faced due south, and the sunny old-fashioned garden was reckoned a fortnight earlier than any other in those parts, so unusually favoured was its situation."

There is nothing ravishing about this ; no suggestion of great excitement, but the peace of the English countryside ; that peace which no other country quite seems able to produce—at least from the point of view of the average Englishman !

A great deal has been written by a great many different kinds of people deploring the vices of a solitary life. It has been said, and with a certain amount of truth, that such a condition tends to an outlook which is the reverse of useful. A solitary life has been condemned as a life of entire self-absorption, while these critics have been blissfully oblivious that the nearest approach to God has often been obtained by those who have led the most solitary of lives.

It is said, and again it is said with truth, that man's place is among men, that humanity thrives upon contact with humanity, but it is quite forgotten that Christ probably found his own soul more effectually in the Wilderness than in the rush of the crowded streets of Jerusalem. Again it is said that a too solitary life tends to a distorted imagination, vague and unreasoning fears, it is forgotten that the solitary individual is more often entirely at peace with himself and with the humanity he wisely prefers in the abstract.

Such a character appears to have been the lovable old Vicomte in Mrs. De La Pasture's book. To him his solitary life appears to have been but a quiescent passage, something guiding his soul along so quietly that the journeying is scarcely noticeable.

" He lived so solitary a life that the past and present had become almost one to him, and time fled over his whitened head unheeded."

Such perhaps is a state as near to contentment as can be obtained by mortals. No unreasoning regrets for the past and no haunting fears for the future. Mrs. De La Pasture puts the " philosophy of content " accurately in the few lines I have quoted.

I have already mentioned that Mrs. De La Pasture is

old fashioned enough to describe by description. The actual look of the old Vicomte is given by this manner of writing. Again, it is the type of description that has very largely been eliminated by present day novelists. Whether this is a virtue or a vice is a matter of opinion.

" In person the Vicomte was of immense size, and his bushy eyebrows, and fierce white moustache and imperial gave him a military appearance."

Mrs. De La Pasture denotes his deportment with an apt simile, it is a sentence almost modern !

" He moved with something like the elegant shuffle of a dancing master."

But, he appears to have avoided the colossal conceit of that kind of person.

" But the politeness of his manner, combined with a perfect simplicity, suggested, nevertheless, the foreigner of distinction."

In these few lines we get really all we need to know about the appearance of this old-world figure. There is certainly quite a good deal to be said for this description by description, even if it be contended that there is much more to be said for description by suggestion.

There is a very delightful passage written by Mrs. De La Pasture when she narrates a discussion between the two grandchildren of the Vicomte. It displays the artlessness and ingenuity of children which they employ when engaged upon the difficult and embarrasing pursuit of knowledge.

" Why is the moon so faded in the afternoon ?" asked Kitty, pointing with a fat forefinger to the cloudless sky."

The answer to this highly scientific question is in Mrs. De La Pasture's most exquisite manner.

" ' You can't expect it to shine day and night, child,' said her sapient elder ; and she hammered joyfully at the door in the west wall."

Most children invest the moon with human qualities, most children think that it sleeps during the day ; or how could it shine so brightly through the nursery windows ; how could it watch all night all the sleeping children in all the world, if it had to watch all day ? Besides, the moon is kind ; it would not want to claim attention when it was the time for the sun to be in the public eye ! This reply about the moon being liable to fatigue shows a keen understanding of the child mind.

But there is something far more important than the faded moon ; a tea party in preparation, the most exciting thing in the world when we are very young and merely a painful duty when we are very old. For when we are grown up, if we can pay for them, we can eat as many cakes as we like, but when we are young it is only at a tea party that the number of cakes to be eaten are not limited. In fact we can be grown up, how ironic when we are grown up, we know we can never be children at a tea party again. Yet there is no one to say—" No more cakes, or you will be sick," but the cakes have lost their wonderful flavour.

Mrs. De La Pasture gives us something of the delights and fears of a coming tea party.

" ' Is it a tea party, grandpapa?' cried Kitty, hastily disengaging herself from his arms, to gaze in rapture at the well-known preparations for a coming feast on the lawn.

" ' It is a tea party, for there is Odo,' said Rosaleen ; ' and it is always a tea party when Odo comes.'

" ' Or there wouldn't be enough to eat,' said Kitty, innocently. "

Mrs. De La Pasture mentions an idea which is, in some ways, peculiarly an American notion. It may be the essential reason why America has achieved such an astonishing success in such an astonishing short time. We may, and many of us do, dislike the idea in England, but the virtue of it must be considered. It is a remark that " the man from America utters," in reply to an affirmation by the Vicomte.

" ' I have heard that, in America, young men know more than their parents.'

" ' Every generation ought to know more than the last, sir, and always has done so,' said Mr. Brett unabashed."

It is true enough that every generation should endeavour to acquire more real knowledge than the last ; it is highly questionable whether each generation has lived up to this high ideal. In discussing this question we should be embarking upon the highly controversial subject of progress, and it is no part of this Essay to do so. Let it be then merely said that I believe, however far it may fail, that America is trying to let each generation progress in knowledge farther than the one that preceded it.

But this question of the next generation knowing more than the last is seldom pleasing to old people. It is not conceit, but simply that the maturity of old age mistakes the enthusiasm of youth, its apparent irresponsibleness, its slightly veiled irritation with the ideals of the generation that gave it birth. Mrs. De La Pasture appears to equally realise the point of view of the young American and the conservative old French aristocrat. It is a far seeing piece of psychology, coupled with a ready sympathy.

"'In my young days, sir, I who speak to you,' said the Vicomte with emotion, 'honoured my parents, and did not venture to dispute their opinions.'"

Perhaps if there is one thing that old people do not realise, it is that opposition or a contradictory opinion to that of a parent, is not, *ipso facto*, a lessening of respect, a loss of affection on the part of the child. Rather, it is that the young generation not only wishes to learn from its parents, it wishes to make practical use of that learning, by supplementing.

Old people do not perhaps wish to supplement, youth by its very nature nearly always does.

Mrs. De La Pasture deals very frankly with the very outspoken questions that children address to other people ; questions that have in them no hint of hypocrisy, for a child is never hypocritical. The question arises when the grand-children, not knowing the true circumstances, imagine that "the man from America" has taken all the Vicomte's fortune. There is some delicious dialogue.

"'Daddy says the man from America took away all bon papa's money,' she said calmly. 'Did you ?'

" Mr. Brett's grey eyes seemed to take fire. Then he smiled rather queerly.

" ' Never mind,' said Mr. Brett gently. ' If the man from America took your grandpa's money away, I guess he'll bring it back.' "

It demonstrates the good sense of a grown up person who refuses to be offended by the direct questionings of a young person.

So far we have been discussing Mrs. De La Pasture as the creator of pleasant characters, people we cannot help liking, people whose presence brings with it a sense of joy, and a pleasure. But she is equally skilful in creating the opposite kind of person—people whose absence is a very great delight. Mrs. Trethewy unfortunately is no uncommon type of individual, mean in spirit and full of a vicious delight in counting all the halfpennies which have no right to be counted, but come from the Mint to be spent. Not content with annoying other people, Mrs. Trethewy annoys herself !

" She was determined that her servants should get the worst of everything at the least possible expense to herself. She was for ever counting halfpence, suspecting short weight, and pouncing upon abuses in the back premises ; and she appeared content to sacrifice her own leisure and peace of mind to her resolve that her domestics should enjoy neither."

There is no condition more likely to produce a two-edged sword than that which is carping and always zealous to find fault.

Mrs. De La Pasture makes the Vicomte something of a philosopher, something of a sophist. He enunciates a really very wise saying about the very usual worship that is accorded to riches.

" ' The vulgar, my son, have a respect for riches which they do not always accord to virtue.' "

To which there is a sharp but not entirely untrue retort.

" ' That is so Vicomte, but riches are harder to get.' "
It might be added that they are certainly harder to keep !

.   .   .   .

The work of Mrs. De La Pasture abounds with these rather smart but not superficial sayings, of which the one I have quoted is pre-eminent.   They fall from the lips of those who utter them ; they are not clever sayings said by dull and stupid people.   The naïvete of the children and the sophistication of the grown-ups form a distinct contrast. They prove Mrs. De La Pasture to be an observer of life at both ends, of life in society and very much out of it.

Mrs. De La Pasture takes a lot of trouble with her characters.   Not only does she let us see what they understand, she is equally persevering to let us observe what they do not.   Thus, the old Vicomte does not understand that his grandchildren have grown tired of the quiet life of the country and want to see something of the marvels of London.   The scene is rather a pathetic one, as the old man is very much dismayed by the demands of his grandchildren.

" It may seem nothing to you, grandpapa.   But when you think we have never even been to London ! We know not a word of German or Italian ; we have had no dancing or gymnastic lessons ; our frocks are all wrong ; and we have never stayed at an hotel in our lives.' "

But even if the old Vicomte has been a *little* thoughtless in isolating the children so much, when he reflects, he realises that the point of view of old age and the point of view of youth are very, very different.

" But they had yet to buy their own experience in the matter ; and the conclusions to which their grand-father had come at the end of his life were not very likely to impress them whilst they were still at the beginning of their own."

So we shall be forced to leave the sweet peace of Devon and follow the Vicomte and his grand children through some of the intricacies of a London season.

.   .   .   .

When the Vicomte and his grandchildren get to London we get some gorgeous dialogue with an old London " cabby." Dear old cabbies. I suppose most of them have driven their last journey, but may the soil rest very lightly on their bones. On the whole they were a good-natured crowd, a good deal better than the supercilious taxi-drivers of to-day, who too often snarl when they are asked to drive somewhere and snarl when they are well paid for so doing.

Mrs. De La Pasture gets the atmosphere of the old London cab driver remarkably well.

" Returning dejectedly, she told the expectant occupants of the cab that the second act of the play was nearly over, and that the man could not promise them good seats. The driver was quite concerned at this third disappointment, as he opened the door for her to re-enter the cab.

" ' Lor bless you, miss, what kin yer expec ? It's

close on arf parse nine. There's a time to think of
going to a pop'lar play as begins at hate o'clock. Why
don't yer go to the 'alls ? You'll be just right for the
best turns.' "

No, we don't get this kind of conversation now ; we are
too sophisticated ; we could never spare time to discuss
the coming evening's amusement with a cabman ; with
an air of patronising condescension we tell the chauffeur
to drive to such and such a theatre, where is to be seen the
play and players who have been so highly praised by the
dramatic critics that all suburbia is there, with its fat
underdressed women and its fat overdressed men. As
for the " halls," they hardly exist ; the cinema has cruelly
pushed them out. The London of Mrs. De La Pasture is
dead, but, unlike the mortal dead, it will never rise again.
We may get new lamps for old ones, but we do not get
old cities again when once the new ones have crept in.

If the London cabman is at one extreme of society,
society itself is at the other extreme. If there is one
criticism which can be fairly levelled at that fraction of
London which calls itself " society," it is that there is
nearly always an air of insincerity about the people who
constitute it. They are neither bad nor good ; they are
for the most part artificial people whose whole standard of
life consists in either a violent conservatism or a repulsive
attempt to the breaking of all moderate conventions.

Thus you get a number of quite interesting parties at
which some discerning host or hostess introduces a
novelty. But for the most part society is bored, it has
no conception of the meaning of life, it rushes rather aim-
lessly from one mechanical function to another, it merely
touches the surface of things, yet society has a glamour

and a magnetism that makes nearly all the rest of the universe regard it with either amused contempt, passionate anger or deadening envy and jealousy.

Mrs. De La Pasture gives some very true pictures of this curious phenomenon which is society ; she exposes its inanities, its lack of any reality ; yet, in my opinion, she gives also the subtle attraction of it.

There is a good description of bored society when the grandchildren attend an afternoon tea party at the house of Lady Domaford.

" Lady Domaford stood just inside the largest of the communicating reception-rooms in her town house, and languidly greeted her thronging guests as they entered. She looked as bored as she felt, for this was her *omnium gatherum* party, intended to soothe the feelings of all the outsiders whose names disfigured her London visiting-list, as well as to please and flatter any country neighbours who might be in town at this time of year, and who were not sufficiently distinguished to be asked on more important occasions."

Lady Domaford is quite evidently a thoroughly objectionable person, for she is patronising and merely interested in distinguished people. With delightful skill Mrs. De La Pasture creates Lord Domaford, the genial peer who is genial because popularity is pleasant and quite often paying. He is the exact opposite to Lady Domaford. He is something of an " artist," and watches his wife's deficiencies so that they may be remedied by the applications of his own most excellent graces.

" Lord Domaford, whose attentive eye was ever upon his wife, hurried forward to supplement her coolness by his own extra warmth.

" ' My dear good creatures, how delighted I am to
see you !' he cried, shaking hands heartily with father,
mother, son and daughter in turn."

Lord Domaford is not quite sincere ; rather a characteristic of very genial people ; but they are so much more
pleasant than those who are sincere and gruff at the same
time.

" He had found this mode of address an excellent one
in cases where his memory for names and identities was
at fault."

It is impossible to hurt people more than not to know
them, and quite evidently Lord Domaford did not intend
to take this risk. Even if Lord Domaford is not quite
sincere, Lady Domaford is most certainly a female pig !
Mrs. De La Pasture comments on her swine-like qualities.

" She belonged to the order of persons who make
it a rule to draw attention to what is blameable, and
are silent concerning what is praiseworthy in their
fellow creatures ; and, who, strangely enough, ascribe
the habit to honesty rather than to a grudging spirit."

If we look for it we can probably always find something
praiseworthy among those we come across. If we cannot
then it is perfectly easy to be silent, for unexpressed
thoughts do no harm except to the soul, and it is our fault
if we injure that.

A little further on in their progress through the London
season we are introduced to another very clever bit of
dialogue put into the mouth of Lord Domaford. It
demonstrates something of the rather snobbish attention
that is paid by certain " thrusters " to royalty. The
incident is when Lord Domaford insists that the Vicomte

cannot leave without supper, when as a matter of fact the peer is only concerned for the royalty that are present.

" ' My dear good man,' said Lord Domaford, fussily, ' you must not go without supper. I insist—I implore— nay, I would come with you myself—but you will understand '—he lowered his voice—' His Royal High- ness—I must be on duty until he leaves. He probably won't stay very long.' "

But the Vicomte is not easily hoodwinked. There is a very pathetic piece of writing when the old man looks back on something that was before the coming to London and will never be the same again. Mrs. De La Pasture pours out much sympathy on the old Vicomte. A fairly long quotation will show the delicate picture of the sad old man.

" He was growing very old, and felt as though his beloved little ones were somehow slipping from his grasp. Their childhood had faded into the past, together with his own youth—and the friends, and the feasting, and the fighting of his youth. The angelic babes he had cherished were gone for ever, and in their place stood two mortal maidens, holding out their white arms to life, with their fair faces turned away from him, and their bright eyes gazing gladly into the future. To-night he had felt himself like a ghost, looking on at a strange world which had succeeded his own dead world, and with which he had nothing at all in common."

London with all its bustle and callousness is no place for the gentle old nobleman.

" ' It is time,'' thought the Vicomte, dismally, ' that I went back to my hermitage at Honeycott, where these sad thoughts did not afflict me, and where I could occupy myself with my garden and the making of my soul.' "

But there is a bitter realisation, that though the old may pine to leave the roar and glare of London, those who are young will never be content to be away from its bustle for very long. For the young soul is fed on the noise of a vast city, the indescribable hum of millions of beings, the subtle feeling that *this* is the centre of the whole world.

At the end of " The Man from America " there are some lines which have a quiet simplicity about them.

" The Vicomte filled himself a bumper of the Madere sec, and drank it, standing alone at the table.

" ' *A la memoire de ma jeunesse !*' said old Patrick—and reversed the glass."

. . . .

" The Man from America " is Mrs. De La Pasture at her best. Pathos, humour and satire work in an artistic harmony. The writing of this authoress is certainly old-fashioned ; the people in her books seem to have disappeared. But in this book that attempts to deal with some of the prominent women novelists of our own time, Mrs. De La Pasture has her place. It is a place that will always be accorded to the novelist who is the quiet teller of a story.

There is a certain wistfulness about Mrs. De La Pasture, for she writes of life that has gone. Modernism has changed so much ; whether for better or for worse, is a matter that each individual has to decide for himself. Of the novelists of whom I have attempted to write a discussion, Mrs. De La Pasture is perhaps more than any of them, a describer of the civilisation that was swept away by the war.

PART EIGHT
MRS. BAILLIE-REYNOLDS

MRS. BAILLIE-REYNOLDS
Press Portrait Bureau.

PART EIGHT

MRS. BAILLIE-REYNOLDS

MRS. BAILLIE-REYNOLDS combines the art of telling a good story with the art of creating characters who attract us by their virtue and repel us by their vice. Yet, strange is the psychology of human liking, the bad characters are really quite attractive, they are so clever, so human, so much like ourselves !

In this Essay, which attempts to say something about Mrs. Baillie-Reynolds, a novel which can only be described as a thriller has to be discussed. Mrs. Reynolds knows exactly how to write this engaging kind of fiction, this fiction which grips with a relentless grip, this fiction which drives us into a secluded corner where we hope that life for an hour or so will be quite unaware of our existence. Mrs. Reynolds makes us desire solitude, not because we hate our fellow men, not because we selfishly wish to avoid human contact, but because we wish to enter fully into the exciting and breathless world which has been constructed for us. The thriller has a distinct mission, it tries to convert the commonplace surroundings of everyday life into a hotbed of trap doors, sudden revolver shots, smart meals with smart villains, unshaved ruffians who speak with a very foreign accent, women who are so beautiful that their execrable morals and disgraceful feminine wiles have to be forgiven.

. . . .

From the many delightful books that Mrs. Baillie-Reynolds has given us I have chosen one which she has called " Lost Discovery." It is a curious medley of love and crime, a very complex study of cross purposes. In this book Mrs. Reynolds is in a mood when she wants to carry us along so breathlessly that the progress leaves us wondering where the journey is going to end—how it is going to end. Mrs. Reynolds is something more than the writer of an admirable thriller ; she has that most necessary gift for the writer of fiction of the thrilling kind, a keen grasp of human nature. Mrs. Reynolds never by any chance creates puppets, she knows only too well that we have no care if a puppet is shut up in a dark dank cellar, but she knows only too well that we are desperately miserable when the ominous clang shuts the beautiful adventuress in the dismal cellar.

The characters in " Lost Discovery " are sensible people, even if many of them are distinctly unpleasant and the reverse of genial. They postulate the fact that it is always impossible to know what another person is really thinking unless he chooses to tell you. They postulate another fact which will never be destroyed ; that in all circumstances what people really care about is love.

Althea Kempthorne, the principal character in " Lost Discovery," is an attractive person who hates the idea of getting at all old ; she is one of those people who can be seen in almost any boarding house—a little nondescript, longing all the time for a lover, so that the boarding house shall be exchanged for a husband and a home.

When the book opens Althea is a little depressed. She has perhaps good reason to be so ; for a woman she is getting a little old. Mrs. Reynolds puts the matter quite clearly if somewhat crudely.

" Only yesterday she had been in the depths of depression.; and this for two good reasons. In the first place it was her twenty-fifth birthday, and for the first time she was reflecting that birthdays are milestones."

But there is something more insistent that caused her depression ; something that means, you do not know quite what the future is to be.

" And in the second place, she had lost her job."

In this direct manner Mrs. Reynolds shows a knowledge of the common causes that create depression. Nothing is perhaps more depressing than the loss of a job, even if the job has not been as delightful as it might have been. Being a government official, Miss Kempthorne had lost her job through a burst of economy. Such then is the background from which Mrs. Reynolds evolves her story.

Mrs. Reynolds seems to have a distinct understanding of the feminine mind, that mind which is annoyed when a man does not wish to make friends. It is a little curious this ; the kind of non-reciprocity which seems to exist so often between the sexes. A man likes a woman ; she takes no notice of him ; he is vaguely annoyed. The same man is liked by another woman ; he takes no notice of her ; she is vaguely distressed. In so many fundamentals, in so many emotions, the sexes appear to experience the same annoyances, the same disharmonies, the same subtle suggestion that life likes to create discords, hopeless likings, painful disillusions.

Althea is vaguely annoyed that one of the young men in her boarding house does not show any marked signs of wishing to be friendly. It is something of a blow to the natural conceit that pervades all girls who cannot imagine for a moment how they can be of no interest to that nice but reserved young man, who does not buy them chocolates or even *suggest* taking them out.

Garnon is this kind of elusive male who knows the best way to attract a woman is to take no notice of her.

" Garnon had arrived at the hotel the previous spring. He was of attractive appearance, but too reserved to be popular. Althea supposed that she never thought of him at all ; but in reality her idea of him was coloured by the instinctive resentment a woman can never help feeling for a man who looks nice and will not make friends."

Probably Garnon knew only too well that it is impossible to be " friendly " with a woman ; it has never been accomplished and never will be. After all, Adam's friendship for Eve did not do him much good. You can be friendly with your own sex, but the emotion is too static to be employed when the other person is the other sex.

But Garnon is not quite indifferent to Althea. Mrs. Reynolds writes some light-hearted modern conversation between Althea and Garnon. It is something that is the beginning of a mutual interest between two young people ; that moment when life is beginning to open out into unexpected channels—channels which will lead to delight or blank misery. But we must not proceed too far Garnon has said that he will get an invitation with the same persons with whom Althea is going to stay. The quotation will perhaps show how cleverly Mrs. Reynolds writes of very up-to-date people ; the free and easy kind relationship which for good or evil has come in since the war.

> " He gave her a queer smile. ' Will you bet I don't get it ?'
>
> " This was quite a new presentment of Mr. Garnon, and Althea felt as if she had met him for the first time. Did she wish him to come to Curfew Place or not ? Somewhat to her own surprise, she found herself owning that she would have no objection to his presence there ; and further, that he was the only person at the Beauregard of whom she could have said as much.
>
> " ' Yes, I'll bet,' said she recklessly. ' Even fifties— de Reszke's.' "
>
> " ' Done,' cried the young man swiftly, as, raising his hat, he ran across the road and vanished down a subway."

There is something very natural and very young about this dialogue ; something delightful for it of two people, who, at least for the moment, are finding life sweet and kind.

Not long afterwards we get a different kind of modern conversation ; something that is merely artificial ; the kind of conversation that gets over the time between the soup and the end of the meal—smart inane talk, all that kind of chatter which makes up the murmuring buzz in some large restaurant. Mrs. Reynolds does reproduce it

very cleverly, she has probably listened to it so often.
The party are discussing the country house to which they
all hope to go for the coming Christmas.

" ' And what,' he wished to know, ' will you do there
in the depth of winter ?'

" ' Skate, I hope, if it will be kind enough to freeze.'

" ' And hunt, I hope, if it prefers to thaw,' chimed in
Olive. ' The Arrington's a small hunt, but Lord
Willimind, who runs it, is very go ahead . . . and we've
got a billiard-table for wet days.'

" ' So it doesn't sound as if we should perish with
ennui ?' suggested Althea.

" ' It makes my mouth water,' replied Penrose,
thinking how the lustreless, misty tint of her hair
enhanced the brilliance of her eyes. "

Mrs. Reynolds apart from her skill in writing of
modern conversation, has a gift for description. She has
a knack of writing description in a way which makes us
feel we are actually present, we can see the people in her
descriptions ; we can hear the sounds, we can imagine so
intently, the black wet night, that we are certain that
sound is the rain actually beating against our own windows. There is an admirable picture of a train feeling its
weary way along and through the blackness of a winter
night in dear old East Anglia. There is all the suggestion of nature trying to prevent the inexorable train
getting to its right conversation ; there are the little
stations sleepily waking into a semblance of life when the
train draws in. Then there is the relapse into blank
melancholy when the lights of the train have finally disappeared round the neighbouring curve. Mrs. Reynolds
enumerates all the little details so carefully.

" The black, inexorable darkness of a moonless, wet winter night had fallen over East Anglia as Althea's train pursued its slow way over the final stage of its journey. Rain drove against the carriage windows like the patter of shot, and flowed over the panes as if sluiced from a bucket. The stations at which they continually stopped were half lit, empty, desolate. Passengers alighted—no one entered the train."

I have said that Mrs. Reynolds has the art of writing a thriller. Now perhaps one of the most necessary attributes that go to make up this particular recipe in fiction, is a sense of coming evil : the sudden shiver in the train, the shriek of the wind tearing across a bleak common, the momentary glimpse of an evil and repulsive face. Very skilfully does Mrs. Reynolds suggest coming excitements, coming evils, an atmosphere of hidden danger.

Althea has arrived at her station on the way to the country house for Christmas.

" A chauffeur advanced, touching his cap, and relieved her of what she carried. She was sharply conscious of a face she disliked—clean-shaven, deeply lined, with pale eyes and hair which had been red but was grizzling. As this man took her things, he gave her a look—a swift transitory glance, so trivial as to be over weighted by the words necessary to describe it ; but the kind of look one does not expect from a well trained servant—appraising, critical, arrogant."

There is just enough in this to make us realise that this servant may be something more than a servant, that the swift look conveys a hidden meaning, that there may be some great excitement a bit later. It is the "stage effect" which Mrs. Reynolds knows how to employ so well.

In writing of the conventional church-going Mrs. Reynolds writes something that is profoundly true. It is, of course, even in these advanced days, a habit among certain types of people to attend service on a Sunday morning. There is no more delightful custom. The walk across the fields, or along the quiet lanes, the sleepy old church waking into life with the peal of bells. Then the service with the old rector and the white surpliced choir boys, the well remembered hymns ; it is all so English, so peaceful, even if the actual worship is a little mixed up with lively anticipations of coming hot beef and a good day for hunting on Monday morning. Of course, Sunday morning church-going in the country is a chance to meet neighbours that are not seen all the week, but if so, surely there is not much harm done. The Deity, if He is personal, is surely full of commonsense, and He will not expect the whole attention of a congregation that is human and out of town for a too short week-end. Mrs. Reynolds creates the atmosphere of this church-going quietly and without criticism.

> " ' Church is the rallying ground for the county. We want to introduce you to the M.F.H.—Lord Willimond. His wife's American, and we get on very well.' "

Even if the Church of England is a body which lends a social atmosphere to its worship, it will be a very disastrous day for England, if it should happen that church is not the rallying ground for the county. We may indeed pray that such a day may never come.

It is a long way from the peace of the Sunday morning in the country to a strange nightmare that Althea experiences. Mrs. Reynolds still keeps up the suspense ; the air of mystery deepens, the quick glances become more pronounced, we are not sure whether it was a nightmare or whether it was a reality. Althea narrates the disturbing experiences.

> " ' Here's Althea,' cried Olive, after the greetings were over. ' Been going in for a nightmare, the wildest ever ! She dreamed she tried to go out of her room in the small hours to fetch a book, and found herself shut in by an iron door.' "

Then we get another of the " stage effects " which show that we are in the middle of an intrigue—in the maëlstroom of plot and counter plot.

> " Althea happened to be watching Garnon as this was said, and caught a sudden flash of inquiry, gone as soon as seen."

It is perhaps one of the most noticeable characteristics of Mrs. Reynolds that she gets right into her plot by means of the method of suspense, by the method of creating " possibilities." It is the skill which makes up a plot but which, at the same time, does not give it away.

A little further on, when the plot is becoming more complicated, we have another of these " possibilities." This time it is the meeting between two comparative strangers, and the curious idea that there has been a meeting before, a meeting only mistily recalled.

The dialogue is carefully contrived, the obvious wish of the one man not to have been met before. All this deepens the mystery.

" ' Surely we've met before,' said he, quickly.

" ' I think not.'

" ' You're Swiss, are you not.'

" Garnon smiled. After a slight hesitation, ' My mother was Swiss,' he replied.

" ' Well, then, last year, on the Antwerp boat.'

" ' Some mistake. But I'm a common type, I fear. Men are always saying to me, " I know a fellow just like you !" ' "

Then by means of an aside we get just a slight idea of Mrs. Reynolds as a philosopher ; something about the philosophy of womanhood. It is certainly wise, for woman's real place is the home, when she is the mistress of it.

" Woman to her finger tips, her womanhood had, as is the case with many girls of to-day, been kept, as it were, in cold storage for the past few years. She had been compelled to meet men of her own age and class daily on business terms. Her femininity had been veiled in an office frock and a cut and dried manner."

A very false setting for Althea, as it is for any woman.

" Even at the Beauregard, the need for circumspection of behaviour was never absent. It was long since she had felt, as she felt this Christmas Eve, the sovereignty and ease of the girl upon her own hearthstone— as it were the daughter of the house."

Even greater would have been her sovereignty if she had been the wife and mother of the house. It is sad but true, and I believe it always will be true, that the married woman experiences the reality of womanhood in a degree that the most successful woman in the world never does. Feminists are always striving for a second best, for they have missed the best.

It will be as well to give a quotation from Mrs. Reynolds when she has ceased suggesting a mystery and has actually admitted us to a full view of the climax of the excitement.

> " Nothing stirred. Faintly she thought she could hear sounds of voices or movements on the other side of the iron door, but in the passage all was quiet, and she made a bound for the safety of her own room."

Mrs. Reynolds knows how to describe the actual moment of acute danger, the moment when Althea is in deadly peril.

She deals with the actual danger as easily and as skilfully as the various suggestions of coming dangers as I have already indicated.

> " She was just entering when two hands of iron gripped her from behind, and a raucous voice cried :
> " ' Got yer !—Jezebel ! Got yer !'
> " She found herself writhing in the grip of Grote, the chauffeur."

Strangely enough, now and again Mrs. Reynolds falls into the use of the banal. A short extract will make this clear.

> " Although she went in mortal fear of this wicked man (Grote) she had felt herself really safe, in spite of his bluster."

There is a touch of the commonplace and a slight crudity in this suggestion of a black stage villain. Mrs. Reynolds seems for the moment to have lost her skill. Mrs. Reynolds is much more skilful when she is less direct, when she is leading up. Perhaps in a limited sense the approaches to her plots are better than the plots themselves, but this is quite a common fault of " thrilling " fiction. We are led to expect so much, the signals point to such a terrific plot, that when it comes, though it may be excellent, it seems to fall short owing to our preconceived notions of what it is actually going to be.

.   .   .   .

It would be hard to find a more modern novelist than Mrs. Baillie-Reynolds. All her characters are essentially of this twentieth century. They dash here and there in motor cars, their conversation is that conglomeration of English and jargon which is so great a part of our own time.

As the teller of a good story Mrs. Reynolds deserves high praise. Generally speaking, her characterisation is on nearly as high a level. She can write exciting fiction without producing grossly exaggerated fiction. " Lost Discovery," from which I have taken several extracts, is, in my opinion, quite characteristic of Mrs. Reynolds.

It is not only a thrilling story, it is also a little bit of a philosophy. It shows that one girl is cleverer than two men, though it seldom happens that one girl is cleverer than one man. The gradual leading up to the plot is of more interest than the actual plot itself. Mrs. Reynolds seems to devote the bulk of her energy to taking us on a journey to the centre of a plot, then, even if we come away a little disappointed, we must not blame her. For we have expected a little too much very probably.

Mrs. Reynolds is something of a preacher. She has several sensible things to say about women, which is somewhat unusual in these days ! No doubt she would be termed a reactionary, which is exactly why she manages to be quite sensible in her " preachings."

She appears to demand that the most natural place for woman is the home. Her girl in " Lost Discovery," though independent, is all the time longing to be dependent.

Mrs. Reynolds' " villain " is moderately well thought out, but he is probably too violent to be really at all subtle.

" Lost Discovery " ends on a rather happy conventional note, but if so, it merely proves that Mrs. Reynolds understands the delicate art of fiction. It is very difficult not to finish one of Mrs. Reynolds' books, when once it has been begun. This is the key to her art, the spell that she casts over the reader.

Mrs. Baillie-Reynolds is, in the much hackneyed use of the phrase, a clever novelist. That is, she attracts the reader, she enlists his sympathy and his anger, she combines murder and passion with delicate love and romance. In some ways she is one of the most " readable " women novelists of this particular time.

The eight novelists that are written of in this book show fiction to be a very wide and comprehensive form of art.

They have perhaps one thing in common. All these novelists write that a sad world may be amused, thrilled and led for a small space of time away from everyday realities.

I would not predict that any of these novelists will survive their death by many years. But fiction for the most part cannot hope for immortality. It is written for the amusement of mortals and is by its very nature mortal.

I have called these writers of fiction " goddesses " ; not because they should be worshipped, but because they deal with Art ; which is to say that Art with condescension and kindliness has invested them with a Divine spark—thus making them goddesses.

I do not believe that any of them are unworthy of the Divine condescension !

DATE DUE

GAYLORD			PRINTED IN U.S.A.